PRAISE FOR THE
Curious Encounters of the Human Kind
SERIES

"Most of Paul Sochaczewski's curious encounters start out as intelligent travel writing, exploring hidden corners of Asia and characters very much out of the ordinary. But this series works on a more complex level: he frequently zooms in and out of left field with a curious tangent, a sensitive reminiscence, a provocative opinion, a new way of looking at events that already are beyond most 'normal' travelers' tales. I read each story feeling refreshed, enlightened, and curious to see what the next stage of Sochaczewski's journey would bring."

—JUDITH M. HEIMANN, author of *The Most Offending Soul Alive: Tom Harrisson and His Remarkable Life* and *The Airmen and the Headhunters: A True Story of Lost Soldiers, Heroic Tribesmen and the Unlikeliest Rescue of World War II*

"What a discovery! Paul Sochaczewski is that rarest of writers who knows that the real 'Asian miracle' isn't malls or computer geeks. In his years traveling the continent, he has discovered an eternal assemblage of arcane explorers, putative emperors, frivolous mystics, sacrosanct elephants and, yes, miracle workers. When Sochaczewski finds them, in Javanese palaces or sacred forests protected by spirits, they are caviar (or sweetened bird's nest) for his fascinating portraits. A book for everyone who knows that the Mysterious East is alive and well, and more how-about-that-wonderful than you perhaps imagined."

—HARRY ROLNICK, author of *The Chinese Gourmet, The Complete Book of Coffee,* and *Spice Chronicles: Exotic Tales of a Hungry Traveler*

"Paul Sochaczewski skips about Asia like a Monkey God hopping from mountain to mountain, bringing back life-prolonging peaches while annoying the gatekeepers. Whatever you do, follow him on this journey!"

—LEE CHOR LIN, director of the National Museum of Singapore; former curator of Asian Civilizations Museum – Singapore; author of *Batik: Creating an Identity*

"Sochaczewski is a world-class searcher, reporter, and observer who has criss-crossed Asia for forty years, pausing in the most unlikely places and finding extraordinary people. The essays in this insightful and witty chronicle present a rich tapestry of eccentric nobles, self-serving naturalists, scoundrels who will make your teeth ache, celebrity monks, and memorable folks whose stories are too good to be true. But they are."

—CHRISTOPHER G. MOORE, author of the Vincent Calvino novels and *Heart Talk*

"In this series Sochaczewski explores the hidden corners, the forgotten people, and their surprising tales. All the personal traveler's tales in these volumes are captivating, all filled with humor, drama, and insight, with an edgy take-no-prisoners voice. You won't find anything else like this on the bookshelf."

—JEFF MCNEELY, chief scientist, International Union for Conservation of Nature

"The *Curious Encounters of the Human Kind* series is a delicious stew of improbable characters and intriguing stories, served up in thoroughly pithy style, and with a hearty dash of irreverent humour."

—TIM HANNIGAN, author of *Raffles and the British Invasion of Java* and *Brief History of Indonesia: Sultans, Spices, and Tsunamis: The Incredible Story of Southeast Asia's Largest Nation*

"Constructed on a base of strange but true personal travel adventures, *Curious Encounters* adds elements of history, an edgy sense of humour, mysticism, political incorrectness, current affairs, and memorable characters you'll wish you had the pleasure to meet on your travels. Consider each book in this series like a good curry – the result is more than the sum of its parts; each tale has its own zing. Travel with these books to the little-visited corners of Asia, and savour them.

—JASON BROOKE, director of The Brooke Trust

"I never tire of living vicariously through Paul Sochaczewski and his writing adventures. He keeps finding these wonderful details that miraculously open up entire worlds to be explored. Paul is the last of the Great Hunters, only instead of trophies, it is stories he brings home for our admiration, wonder, and delight."

—MARK OLSHAKER, Emmy-winning filmmaker;
author of *Einstein's Brain*, *The Edge*, and *Mindhunter*

"The *Curious Encounters* series is proof positive that a writer/ traveler can immerse himself in Asian cultures and yet remain objective enough to write extremely entertaining and often irreverent articles and colorful stories about what he has experienced. From Indonesian mystics to Burmese white elephant hunters, the descriptions are spot-on. There is something in these articles and stories that reminds me of the writing of Paul Theroux – not as cynical, perhaps, but the author is just as able to look at events with a clear, unsentimental and yet sympathetic eye. You won't regret a moment spent reading these tales, which perfectly capture the allure and spice of the places visited."

—DEAN BARRETT, author of *Memoirs of a Bangkok Warrior*

Volumes in the

Curious Encounters of the Human Kind

series:

Myanmar (Burma)

Indonesia

Himalaya: India, Bhutan, Nepal

Borneo

Southeast Asia:
Thailand, Laos, Cambodia, Vietnam, the Philippines

Other Titles by Paul Sochaczewski

Share Your Journey

An Inordinate Fondness for Beetles

The Sultan and the Mermaid Queen

Redheads

Distant Greens

Eco-Bluff Your Way to Greenism

Soul of the Tiger

CURIOUS
ENCOUNTERS
of the
HUMAN KIND

MYANMAR
(BURMA)

CURIOUS
ENCOUNTERS
of the
HUMAN KIND

MYANMAR (BURMA)

*True Asian Tales of
Folly, Greed, Ambition
and Dreams*

PAUL SPENCER SOCHACZEWSKI

EXPLORER'S EYE PRESS

GENEVA, SWITZERLAND

Cover photo: Young girl at the Zee-O Thit-Hla sacred forest, protected by *nat* spirits.

All photos by Paul Sochaczewski, except where noted.

ISBN: 978-2-940573-01-1

Published by:
Explorer's Eye Press
Geneva, Switzerland

Book design by Stacey Aaronson
Map of Myanmar/Burma by John Welding

Printed in the United States of America

Dedicated to the people of Asia who shared their stories,
and sometimes their homes, rice wine, termite omelets,
and dreams.

TABLE OF CONTENTS

AUTHOR'S NOTE

Some thoughts about change in Myanmar:

Is the country called Burma or Myanmar? Journalists, diplomats, and human rights activists have jitterbugged with this question for years. The military junta changed the country's name to Myanmar from Burma in 1989. Some feisty foreign observers, including for varying amounts of time the United Kingdom, the United States, and me, insisted on using the name Burma as shorthand to signal a protest against what they saw as a repressive military-led regime, as then-U.S. Secretary of State Condoleezza Rice did in 2005 when she named Burma an "outpost of tyranny." However, today most foreign observers (including the UN) accept that a country has the right to call itself anything it wants. And within the country, virtually all English language publications, NGOs, businesses, and individuals use the name Myanmar.

I'll use the name Myanmar and accept spelling changes of major locations (Rangoon becomes Yangon, Pagan becomes Bagan). But whatever you call it, Myanmar is undergoing political, economic, and social change that might significantly alter the future of the country. Most noticeably, the country is gingerly experimenting with a form of democracy; it remains to be seen how this awkward shift from military to civilian rule will evolve.

Related, the country's leaders still have to deal with restive ethnic armies, religious and communal violence pitting Buddhists against Moslems, and human rights abuses of Rohingya and Moken minorities. Social patterns too are slowly changing, brought on by a modest amount of foreign investment, an increase in inbound tourism, the presence of foreign journalists, and improved communications, such as satellite dishes and cell phones in urban areas.

Yet vast swatches of Myanmar remain poor and rural, and in terms of criteria of the type taken for granted in neighboring Thailand – roads, electricity, sanitation, health care, education, access to the cash economy – Myanmar remains among the UN's "least developed" countries.

Nevertheless, the people of Myanmar, although they might be cash poor, are proud, honest, and culture-rich, and a visitor is welcomed generously.

Like other countries in the region, Myanmar is trying to figure out how to manage its rich biodiversity (ranging from snow-topped mountains to coral reefs) in ways that will provide income now, yet ensure they will still be around for the next generation. Sometimes this brings Myanmar into conflict with big neighbor China, a country keen to profit from large hydroelectric dams, as well as trade in wildlife, timber, and minerals.

And for me, Myanmar is arguably the most mystical of Southeast Asian nations. The spirits, emanations of animistic creations, specialist *nats*, transgender mediums, and tales evolved from elaborate Buddhist, Hindu, and Christian rituals are rarely far from anyone needing advice and support.

In a very few instances, the reader may find some details outdated because several chapters, in simpler versions, have appeared over a period of twenty years in The *New York Times, International Herald Tribune, Wall Street Journal, Destinasian, GQ, CNN Traveller, Travel and Leisure, Geographical, Reader's Digest*, and other publications.

But while statistics might change, the basic truth of the human stories offered here of foibles, ambitions, and achievements remains constant.

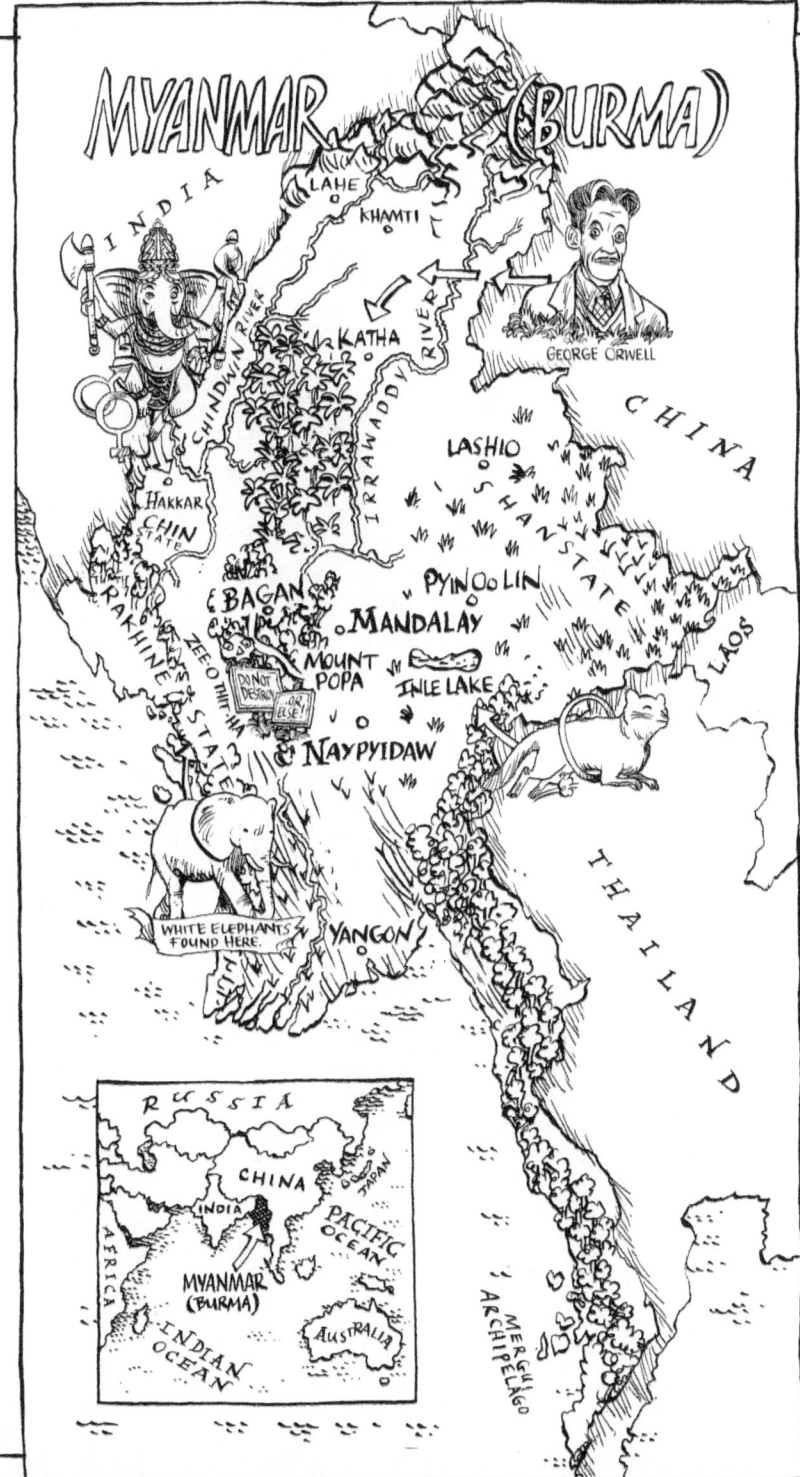

Is training cats one way to achieve the Middle Path?

JUMPING THROUGH
THE BUDDHIST HOOPS

Tina Turner does it, Tom Cruise does it, so does Arnold.
Is the Middle Path suitable for trained felines?

INLE LAKE

"ome on Brochette, jump through this hoop. Arnold Schwarzenegger can do it – it can't be that hard."

Our ginger cat in Geneva was doing what cats every-where do – exactly what she felt like. Which at this moment was not jumping through a hoop.

I was trying to accomplish a similar *coup de persévérance* to that which some monks in Myanmar have achieved. Teaching cats parlor tricks. But Brochette wasn't buying it. What did the monks have that I didn't?

Lots of patience and an abundant supply of Friskies, as it turned out.

I was introduced to the famous Burmese jumping cats at the Nga Phe Kyaung monastery on Inle Lake.

The "jumping cat monastery" is a key stop for the trickle of tourists who visit Myanmar. There I met Venerable U Nanda, 25, one of a dozen resident monks.

"It's easy to train cats," he said, somewhat reluctantly putting down his Burmese comic book. With a large dose of ennui, he explained that you simply start when they're kittens, scratch them under the chin, say *kon*, and reward them with kitty treats.

Obviously, it works. Every thirty minutes or so, when a group of visitors would accumulate, San Win, an assistant in the monastery, would put the cats through their paces.

"What's that one called?" I asked, pointing to a black-and-white tabby.

World-weary U Nanda explained, "That's Leonardo DiCaprio."

"And this one?"

"Demi Moore."

"Can I try?"

I held the wire hoop in front of Arnold Schwarzenegger, paradoxically one of the skinnier cats in the temple. I gave him a little nudge, ordered him to *kon*, and after he jumped I rewarded him with a biscuit.

Meanwhile Tina Turner was curled up on my backpack, asleep. "Don't leave your things on the floor," U Nanda lectured. "She pisses everywhere."

After a while U Nanda started to open up. Perhaps he saw that since I wasn't going to go away, he might as well have a discussion. I was interested in Buddhist history; he was interested in conjugating English verbs.

Throughout our conversation, the abbot, Sayadaw Kite Ti, 68, kept his distance and read a book. I don't read Burmese, but from the pictures of cowboys and horses, I was pretty sure it wasn't a religious text. He didn't glance up as visitors stuffed tattered kyat notes and a few dollar bills into the offering box.

I left Inle Lake to travel around Shan state, and I returned a few weeks later and sought out U Nanda. I felt I had unfinished business with the young monk, a feeling that there was more to him than a saffron-robed, feline-inclined impresario.

"You again," he said when I walked in. He wasn't hostile, but he wasn't overly welcoming.

I deliberately avoided the handful of curious visitors watching Brad Pitt and Michael Jackson leaping about on the linoleum. "Tell me about the temple," I said. And he did. He showed me around the 160-year-old monastery, the oldest on Inle Lake. Proudly, he turned on lights so that I could better see the six two-meter tall Buddha images made out of lacquerware, and the gilt-encrusted wooden statues and carved pillars. He took me into the abbot's room to show me old, sacred Buddha images. In half an hour of looking through different eyes, the monastery for me had evolved from a tourist site into a combination art museum and place of worship.

"What do you do?" he eventually asked me.

"I'm a journalist."

"Then tell people the monastery is more than cats. It's Buddha."

Will this powerful symbol of a just king
bring about a Burmese renaissance?

MYANMAR'S GENERALS HOPE WHITE ELEPHANTS PROVIDE JUMBO SUPPORT

Can rare pale pachyderms make a ruler righteous?

YANGON

ost new national capitals feature monumental architecture, statues to independence heroes, broad boulevards, cultural centers, and shopping malls.

Myanmar's new, deliberately isolated and seldom-visited capital, Naypyidaw, some 320 kilometers north of Yangon, has few of these standard features.

But Naypyidaw (which means "royal capital" in Burmese) may soon have something even rarer and more portentous – a new white elephant. Word around Yangon has it that one of these rare creatures, a male, has been captured and is kept in the Phokyar Elephant Camp in Bogo Division, some 350 kilometers distant. Once an auspicious date can be determined, the animal will be unveiled in the new capital.

It's unclear why Myanmar's ruling generals chose to move the capital from Yangon (the junta changed the city's name to Yangon and the country's name to Myanmar) to Naypyidaw. Some wags say the new, inland capital was selected to protect the petroleum-rich country from an Iraq-like invasion by the United States. Another argument is that centrally located Naypyidaw allows the army a better chance to patrol the restive border regions of the ethnic Shan, Chin, and Karen states. Regardless, an underlying incentive is the belief that a Burmese king (or in this case General Than Shwe, the country's senior leader) could consolidate his power by emulating historic kings, listening to court astrologers who instructed the ruler to create a new capital.

BURMESE RULERS HAVE ALWAYS BEEN IN THE SWAY OF fortune tellers. General Ne Win, who came to power in 1962, was totally dependent on their advice. Fortune tellers told him to change the direction of traffic over-night, which he did, causing huge confusion and numerous accidents. He had a penchant for the number "nine," and in 1987 the government removed the 25, 35, and 75 kyat notes and replaced them with 45 and 90 kyat bills, denominations that could be divided by his favorite number.

Even today, seers determine propitious times for major events. The present military junta began moving government ministries from Yangon to Naypyidaw at exactly 06:37 on 6 November 2005. Five days later, at 11 a.m., a second convoy of eleven hundred military trucks carrying eleven military battalions and eleven government ministries left Yangon.

Myanmar already has three official white elephants, which are on public display in an enclosure near the Yangon airport, guarded by armed soldiers with M16s who politely enforce a "no photography" policy.

The white elephants are fed with fruit from nearby gardens. They spend their days protected from the sun but are nevertheless chained on a tennis-court-sized concrete platform.

Some cynics claim that at least one of the three Burmese white elephants was stolen from a Bangladeshi farmer. In a perhaps apocryphal tale, which is nevertheless told with relish by sophisticates in Yangon, it seems that a Bangladeshi peasant somehow made his way to Yangon, said to the astonished authorities "that's my elephant," and demanded compensation. The Burmese authorities scoffed, asking him to prove his claim. So the farmer spoke to the white elephant in Bengali, the animal responded with a trumpeting of recognition, and the startled authorities gave the man a fistful of U.S. dollars.

WHITE ELEPHANTS HAVE PLAYED A JUMBO-SIZED ROLE in Myanmar's geopolitical ambitions. As U Toke Gale, the country's leading elephant expert, explained:

> The white elephant has always been a symbol of Buddhism, of prestige, prosperity, and political power, and has, at the same time, been for centuries one of the chief causes of invasions and plunder among some countries of the East.

Between 1549 and 1769, for example, the Buddhist kings of Myanmar, Thailand, and Cambodia fought a two-hundred-year series of violent and important battles over, in part, which ruler had the greatest number of pale pachyderms.

The official *New Light of Myanmar* newspaper does not hesitate to predict that the discovery of the country's three white elephants heralded a new era of prosperity. "Throughout history, white elephants emerged during the time of Myanmar kings and governments who ruled the nation discharging the ten kingly duties," the government newspaper reported. "It is said that the white elephant brings peace, stability and prosperity ... a good omen when the State is endeavouring to build a peaceful, modern and developed nation."

To some skeptics white elephants are just animals with recessive genes that give them albino-like characteristics and other curious attributes, like particularly shaped tails and ears, or a white palate or genitals. But to true believers, and to people like Myanmar's military leaders who use the white elephants to legitimize their positions on the top of the hierarchal totem pole, white elephants are true incarnations of Lord Buddha and are as sacred to many Buddhists as a savior born to a virgin is to Catholics.

IF ONE WHITE ELEPHANT IS GOOD LUCK, THEN SURELY A bunch of them would be extraordinarily valuable. So why not breed the animals to select for the characteristics of their recessive genes, as some wildlife experts in Myanmar have suggested?

The answer to this question depends on whether you consider the white elephant to be a genetic abnormality or a heaven-sent omen.

One Burmese veterinarian was removed from her position after publishing a paper describing the genetic malformation of one of the country's white elephants; she now lives in self-exile in the U.K. She was guilty of bestial blasphemy because any suggestion of genetic malformation is anathema to people who consider the white elephant to be a perfect incarnation of Lord Buddha. In discussing the genetics question with a Burmese colleague, he suggested that "instead of saying 'mutation,' it might be better to say 'extra special.'"

I wanted the official government position on the likelihood of a barnyard-like breed-improving program.

THROUGH A FRIEND I OBTAINED A MEETING WITH LT. Col. (retired) U Shu Maung, the general manager (extraction) of Myanma Timber Enterprise, who is responsible for capturing and maintaining the country's white elephants.

To reach his office, I first wandered past offices that seem Dickensian with a tropical touch – sleepy clerks surrounded by disintegrating paper binders filled with the outputs of a few ancient Underwood typewriters.

U Shu Maung is a jolly man who obviously enjoys a comfortable life in Yangon. Sitting in a spacious office decorated with samples of the dozens of types of wood Myanmar produces (much of which is smuggled to neighboring Thailand), he did not hesitate to spin the significance of these rare animals: "Their presence signifies a new Myanmar renaissance," he said.

U Shu Maung explained that the white elephant is a sort of cosmic herald that "only appears during the reign of the righteous leaders." Finding a white elephant is a miracle, he explained, a sign from the heavens, suggesting it would be wrong to think you could preempt the flow of the cosmos by breeding the sacred animals like chickens or buffalos.

More practically, one Yangon-based cynic asked what would happen if they bred two white elephants, and twenty-two months later found they had created an ugly, or even a malformed creature? That would be terrible for the image of a holy pachyderm, and for the image of the sensitive generals and their State Peace and Development Council.

MYANMAR'S THREE WHITE ELEPHANTS, TWO MALES AND a female, were found in the forests of Rakhine state, near the border with Bangladesh. U Saw Sei, the veterinarian who tranquillized the rare animal, relates how nervous he was during the sensitive procedure. "This is heavy duty work," he said, explaining that they couldn't dart the elephant in a swamp or near a river (it might drown) or too close to a steep incline (it could stumble and become injured). "We understood that 'if you don't capture it, don't come back home,'" he said.

I asked U Thaung Nyunt, the assistant manager of Myanma Timber Enterprise who also participated in the capture, what would have happened if his team failed to catch the elephant? Half joking, he ran his index finger under his chin, in a universal sign of "big trouble."

MYANMAR HAS BEEN COLLECTING WHITE ELEPHANTS with alacrity and propitious timing; the country's eighth white elephant was captured just before the elections of 2010, and the animal was hailed by state media as the mark of a successful "democratic transition." The capture of a ninth white elephant was announced in early 2015, also just before a national election and at a time when the country's oft-criticized military was battling ethnic Chinese rebels in the country's northeastern frontier, a dispute framed by state media as a defense of sovereignty.

ONE OF MYANMAR'S FIRST THREE WHITE ELEPHANTS, four-year-old Rati Marlar (Precious Flower), captured at 17:20 on July 18, 2002, is a beautiful animal, with skin the color of pinkish sand, white eyelashes, pearl-colored eyes, five toenails on the front feet and four on the back, and as playful as any youngster. While Precious Flower is clearly special, it is rare that a white elephant is so easily discernible; I was confused when I saw another of Myanmar's white elephants, Raja Gaja Sri Pyitsaya (Graceful and Auspicious Elephant King). To a layman this animal appeared disturbingly ordinary.

The problem, I learned, is that white elephants are rarely white, and it can often be difficult for non-specialists to tell at a glance that they are viewing an incarnation of Lord Buddha.

Which leads to the job description of one of the world's more arcane disciplines: white elephant-determining expert. Interpreting ancient Thai and Burmese texts, these men are charged with discerning whether an elephant is truly "white," and therefore worthy of the king.

HOW DID WHITE ELEPHANTS BECOME SO POWERFUL? Like other key Asian symbols, the long cosmological march of the white elephant mystique has its beginnings in animistic beliefs that were subsequently adopted and adapted by proponents of new religions.

In ancient pre-Hindu, pre-Buddhist times, a white elephant was associated with rain clouds and, like the cobra-inspired Nagas, was a symbol of life and prosperity. It made sense then for Hindu priests to build on this time-proven perception, and elephants were written into Hindu mythology. The four-tusked white elephant Airavata, who rose to the surface when the celestial Sea of Milk was churned, was an elephant Adam, begetting all the elephants that followed. Just as sun-eagle Garuda became the mount of Hindu god Vishnu, the elephant became the steed of Indra, the Hindu god of the heavens.

Subsequent Buddhist teachers built on the already deep-rooted Hindu beliefs. Airavata, they argued, had been an incarnate Buddha (bodhisattva). But raising the stakes even higher, they said that a holy white elephant appeared in a dream to Lord Buddha's mother-to-be, Queen Maya. The future Buddha, in his elephant form, held in his silvery trunk a white lotus flower (the symbol of the yoni, female genitalia). The white elephant uttered a long, drawn-out cry, bowed three times, and touched his forehead to the floor. Then he gently struck Maya's right side and entered her womb. The Queen reported this extraordinary vision to the court astrologers, who divined that she would bring forth a great king or a great seer. Nine months later, Prince Siddhartha was born, the Buddhist equivalent of a virgin birth. Present at the birth was Indra, offering his hair as a gift.

And the connection with the Buddhist kings?

One needs only look at the symbolism surrounding

King Bhumibol Adulyadej of Thailand, the world's longest serving monarch (and owner of eleven white elephants, arguably the most ever of any Buddhist king). He is a much-loved man whom many consider to be semi-divine. He is referred to as Rama IX, and the use of the name "Rama" clearly positions him as an avatar of Vishnu, thereby linking him with both Rama (of Ramayana fame), who was the seventh avatar of Vishnu, and with Buddha, who was Vishnu's ninth avatar. To consolidate the symbolism, King Bhumibol's royal emblem features Garuda (*Krut* in Thai), which is Vishnu's mount. When one sees the Thai Krut on a government building, it signifies that it is under the protection and control of the Vishnu-related king, literally "the king/Vishnu is in the building."

So, following the circuitous but pervasive logic of Hindu-Buddhist belief systems, King Bhumibol (and other Buddhist kings) are related to the most powerful Hindu gods, who themselves are also closely associated with Buddha. The white elephant, which adorned Thailand's flag from 1855 to 1916, is a symbol of that cosmic power, and in the context of Asian Buddhist power-grabs, the monarch with the most white elephants wins.

LIKE ANY RELIGIOUS SYMBOL, PARTICULARLY ONE THAT represents a god-king, a visitor is advised not to make fun of the importance of the white elephant. An entertainment called Wilson's English Circus visited Bangkok in the late nineteenth century and drew a huge crowd by advertising that a real white elephant would participate in the next performance. According to Norwegian traveler Carl Bock:

> ... two clowns came in and began jesting about the white elephant. Then in came a small Indian elephant, appearing as white as snow; not a dark spot could be seen anywhere. But the elephant left white marks on everything he touched. He was chalked all over, and when one of the clowns told the other to "rub his nose against the elephant and he will leave his mark on you," an ominous silence was maintained by the great mass of the people, only broken here and there by a suppressed titter.

The Thais were naturally annoyed that fun was being made of an incarnated Buddha. In the usual Thai way of avoiding open criticism, they merely expressed their confident belief that Wilson would be punished for his disrespect of the Lord Buddha. Several days after the Bangkok fiasco, the impostor elephant died at sea on a trip to Singapore. The too-clever Mr. Wilson suffered from dysentery during the voyage and died almost immediately after landing. The reputation of the true white elephant remained untarnished.

WHILE MYANMAR IS FORTHRIGHT (AND PROUD) ABOUT how many white elephants they have, it is surprisingly difficult to figure out how many of the auspicious creatures live in neighboring countries.

The Thais are protective of the king's white elephants, to the point of being wary of disclosing how many he has. Some sources in the Royal Household in Thailand say that King Bhumibol, who has led his country during six decades of development, has eleven *chang pheuk*. (The Thais distinguish between a *chang samkhan*, an elephant which, according to the ancient guidelines, possesses some of the characteristics of white elephant, and a *chang pheuk*, the honorary title of "lord" that is bestowed once the king accepts a *chang samkhan*.) As evidence perhaps that old rivalries linger, U Shu Maung, who was involved in capturing several of Myanmar's white elephants, says he doesn't believe Thailand has any white elephants. Laos has one, while Cambodia, which paradoxically is undergoing a mini business boom, has none.

World leaders have always sought supernatural and spiritual justification for their rule. In the case of Myanmar's military junta, which lost a 1990 election to Aung San Suu Kyi's National League for Democracy party but refused to relinquish power, the country's powerful generals are not shy about declaring themselves de facto royalty.

Using the equation that ownership of a white elephant equals power and legitimacy, authorities held an elaborate naming ceremony for Myanmar's third white elephant (a command performance for the diplomatic corps and high-ranking officials) on February 12, Myanmar's Union Day. Authorities say that the date was chosen by astrologers, and it is merely a coincidence that the auspicious event coincided with a national holiday that marks Bogyoke

Aung San's short-lived achievement of unifying Myanmar's disparate ethnic groups.

As much as Burmese kings sought the power that white elephants provided, the monarchs were similarly terrified when one of their white elephants fell sick. When his favorite white elephant was dying, nineteenth-century King Thibaw, the last Burmese monarch, desperately bestowed vast treasures on the animal – the elephant's forehead was decked with a spray of diamonds to ward off evil spirits, golden pendants were hung from his ears, and above his gold feeding trough, a mirror specially ordered from France was installed to reflect his glory. Yet the white elephant died. The pundits predicted plagues, floods, and earthquakes. But the real disaster was more prosaic. The British took over Myanmar and deposed the king.

THE LAST TWO BURMESE KINGS, MINDON AND THIBAW, had white elephants. Each holy pachyderm had its own palace, guarded by thirty servants, one of them a minister. As a sinecure, each elephant was granted a province whose revenue it could "eat up."

The Governor of Pegu (now Bago, a city eighty kilometers north of Yangon) noted in a report to King Bodawpaya that a "pure" white elephant captured in 1806 was treated, well, royally. A golden barge escorted by gilded canoes filled with dancers and musicians was sent down the Irrawaddy River (named after Myanmar's version of the sacred white elephant Airavata) to fetch the animal. The elephant was bathed in scented sandalwood and housed in a specially built palace of five golden spires that was inlaid with rubies. Its entire route was lined with live banana and sugar cane trees.

Sir James George Scott, a British civil servant who wrote a classic book *The Burman* under the pen name Shway Yoe, adds that a baby white elephant in Myanmar in the 1850s was suckled by ladies who "stood in a long row outside his palace, and the honour was eagerly sought after, for the creature was a national pride and not merely a royal monopoly." In spite of all the mothers' milk, the Lord White Elephant, as it was called, was hot-blooded and on one occasion killed an Englishman who had ventured too near. The king heard the commotion and enquired what was the matter. When he was told, he expressed great concern – a Lord White Elephant is a repository of good deeds and should not bear the red stain of murder. But the elephant's minister calmed the monarch by saying, "Pray do not be disturbed, paya, it was not a man, only a foreigner."

White elephants are treated with great respect even in modern times. When a white elephant calf was born in Myanmar in the 1950s (the nation's last such blessing – all subsequent white elephants have been wild caught), a chronicler noted: "People of all races ... threw at her feet silver coins ... some people fell on their knees and gave her homage, and many were near to weeping with religious fervour."

IN EARLY 2003, THAILAND AND CAMBODIA NEARLY fought a war when Cambodians took umbrage at an imagined comment made by Thai actress Suvanan Kongying who, according to angry Cambodians, said that Angkor Wat should be returned to Thailand. Students of history know that the animosity between these two neighbors had its peak in the two-hundred-year "white elephant wars." Between 1549 and 1769 the kings of Thailand, Cambodia, and Myanmar fought a series of violent and important battles, partly over which ruler had the greatest number of pale pachyderms.

During a particularly bloody sixteenth-century encounter, Thai King Mahachakrapat demanded that King Ang Chan of Cambodia give the Thais a white elephant as reparation for the 1549 destruction of Prachinburi. After Ang Chan indignantly refused, Mahachakrapat sent in the elephant tanks. But the Thais were soundly defeated in the battle, and Ang Chan gloatingly called the site of the victory "Siem Reap," which means "the defeat of Siam." (Today, Siem Reap is the town closest to the Cambodian Angkor Wat temple complex.) But Mahachakrapat didn't give up – in 1558 he sent a stronger army to Angkor Wat, defeated Ang Chan, and returned with a coveted white elephant.

In mid-2013 Myanmar offered to loan a white elephant to Thailand to mark sixty-five years of bilateral relations. The animal was to have been temporarily moved to the

Chiang Mai Zoo in northern Thailand. The Burmese claimed that Thailand's foreign minister Surapong Tovichakchaikul had made the request of his Burmese counterpart Wunna Maung Lwin. The Thais claimed the suggestion was first tabled by the Burmese. In any case, the Burmese pulled the plug on the loan due to the logistical difficulties involved. That such a loan was even considered was exceptional, considering the two countries' history involving white elephants and the loss of face for the Thais if they had accepted the deal, since it would have positioned Myanmar as a greater White Elephant Super-power. After all, in the sixteenth-century, Thailand fought battles on its western front with Myanmar, and white elephant-related plunder was partly responsible for the creation of Myanmar's national symbol, the golden stupa of Yangon's Shwedagon pagoda.

Accompanied by a friend, who was one of Myanmar's elder statesmen, I strolled around this spectacular structure, which Rudyard Kipling described as "a golden mystery on the horizon – a beautiful winking wonder that blazed in the sun." My friend shielded his eyes from the reflection. "It's said that there is more gold on the Shwedagon Pagoda than in the vaults of the Bank of England," he explained, in awe from both the religious importance of the site and the quantity of gold leaf on the stupa. My companion added that much of Shwedagon's gold was liberated from Thailand during the white elephant wars.

For me, the white elephant wars were an enigma. How could two and a half centuries of bloodshed be consecrated to a symbol of the peaceful Lord Buddha? I wondered if W. Somerset Maugham presciently saw the current state of events when he compared Shwedagon's golden presence to "a sudden hope in the dark night of the soul."

My friend, who has lived through the British colonial period, the Japanese occupation, and a succession of postcolonial governments, thinks the presence of a few white elephants doesn't mean much. "What will be will be," he said, obliquely referring to the future of the much-whispered-about oppressive military regime. "If you meditate and do good work then good fortune will come. You will be judged by your actions."

"IT'S A WHITE ELEPHANT."
"NO IT ISN'T." "IS SO."

The problem is that white elephants are rarely white, and it can often be difficult for laymen to tell at a glance that they are viewing a manifestation of Lord Buddha. What distinguishes a normal elephant from a sacred white elephant?

Jeffrey A. McNeely, chief scientist of the World Conservation Union and co-author of *Mammals of Thailand*, points out that unusual coloring is just one aspect of white elephantness. Most white elephant adjudicators agree that in order for a white elephant to be kosher, it has to have four toenails instead of the normal five (and they should be white), the tail and trunk should be straight and long, the eyes must have pearl-colored eyes with yellow irises enclosed by red rings, and the skin must turn red after having water poured on it rather than becoming darker.

Savet Dhanapradit, a member of Thailand's White Elephant Selection Committee, remembers the complications of his first charge, in the late 1950s:

> We received word at the palace that there was a miraculous elephant at a village near the town of Yala. People who drank water from its trunk were cured of their ills ... But the elephant wasn't perfect ... not so beautiful, but it was very intelligent and mixed well with people. My only objection was that her toenails were not suitable. My bosses and I argued for a month about that animal. In the end I concurred with my superiors and signed the certificate [making the animal a *chang sam-khan*]. Dhanapradit says the even the Royal Stable's top current white elephant, considered the finest beast in generations, is only "80% perfect."

While these deliberations can take on the atmosphere of "how many angels can dance on the head of a pin," there is one rarely observed characteristic that guarantees a fast track to white elephant status. Some ancient texts decreed that a sleeping white elephant must not snore but should emit the gentle sounds of Burmese and Thai classical musical instruments.

NOT AN ALBINO?

So a white elephant is an albino, like a white tiger?

Well, sort of, but not really.

Of course, true albino animals do exist in nature – Snowflake, to cite one famous example, was an albino gorilla, caught in the forests of Equatorial Guinea.

But all the white elephants currently in captivity in Thailand, Myanmar, and Laos, are – at best – sand-coloured, not white. They are standard issue Asian elephants (*Elephas maximus*), not a separate species.

The key lies in their recessive genes.

George Amato, director of conservation and science and senior conservation geneticist at the Wildlife Conservation Society, says their pale color is most likely due to a simple recessive, single-point mutation in the gene for melanin. He refers to this as a leucistic malformation, not albinism, due to an error in DNA replication. Amato likens the white elephant phenomena to that of the more common black leopard. He mentions a human parallel – Amato had an African-American friend who had Nordic-colored skin and light blonde hair, but whose physical features – hair, nose, eyes – were similar to the features of most African-Americans.

FOR THE ANGLOPHONES, A WHITE ELEPHANT IS SOMETHING USELESS AND EXPENSIVE

YES, THERE IS A LINK TO THE PRICELESS ASIAN white elephant and the western expression of something being worthless. This phrase evolved from an ancient Thai custom and has shifted meaning over the years.

Thai kings, like monarchs everywhere, were constantly pestered for jobs and favors by nagging from corrupt and otherwise irritating family and friends who were too close to be slammed into the royal dungeons, but who nevertheless had to be taught a firm lesson, but with Thai-like dignity.

The solution for a particularly pesky brother-in-law? Kill him softly by giving him the honor of looking after one of the king's white elephants, an honor the troublemaker could not refuse.

White elephants, as symbols of Lord Buddha and the property of the king, had to receive royal treatment – the finest sugarcane brought in from distant farms, the freshest fruit, jewelry made of gold and precious stones, and teams of specially selected retainers to bathe and care for the animal.

While this eventually bankrupted the Keeper of the Sacred Royal White Elephant, the practice gave the king two benefits – he got rid of an enemy and in the process had someone else look after one of the largest budget lines in the royal household.

Eventually the English phrase "white elephant" evolved in meaning from being "a great honor you couldn't refuse but that would bankrupt you," to "something that is expensive but worthless."

Moses Samuels sits alone,
while his son Sammy Samuels reads from a prayer book.

MOSES DREAMS OF REVERSING
JEWISH EXODUS IN MYANMAR

Caretaker of Yangon's only synagogue dares to dream.
Will his children go forth and multiply?

YANGON

"h, you want to see Moses Samuels," says Rashid, the front desk manager at a Yangon guest house. "He's an old school friend. He's a Jew and I'm a Moslem, but we all got along just fine. Give him my regards."

I locate Samuels inside Myanmar's only synagogue, busy doing what Jews do well – worrying about the future.

Outside the high-ceilinged, blue-tiled Musmeah Yushua synagogue, mostly-Moslem hardware hawkers and textile merchants – some of whom rent stalls on the property owned by the synagogue – trade and bargain and go about their lives. Inside the synagogue, built in 1886, caretaker Samuels stoically tries to fight the sands of time.

Like Martin Luther King, Samuels has a dream. His hope is that the Jewish community of Myanmar will reverse its declining population and become functional again.

Currently there are just forty-five Jews in the congregation. "We rarely have a minyan," Samuels says, referring to the ten men needed for public prayer on the sabbath. The Jewish community has had no rabbi since 1969, no kosher food (but halal Muslim food is a close replacement), and, since no one in the congregation speaks or reads Hebrew, the Torah only gets chanted when officials from the Israeli embassy in Yangon participate in Sabbath prayers.

Facing these odds, one might accuse Samuels of being guilty of the kind of faith Boswell cynically observed was "the triumph of hope over experience."

Sometimes even the optimistic Samuels fears that his beloved synagogue and Jewish community might become nothing more than a cultural curiosity, as has become the case with the Jewish community in Cochin in neighboring India.

Beginning in the mid-nineteenth century, Sephardic Jewish Iraqis, who traded in teak, rice, coffee, jade, and gold, were encouraged by British colonial authorities to settle in Myanmar. The Jewish community grew and at its peak numbered some twenty-five hundred people.

But most of the Burmese Jews fled at the outset of World War II, while those few who remained sought greener pastures when Myanmar's military government took over in 1962.

Samuels, who was born and bred in Myanmar, hopes that his children will be part of the solution. The only single Jews for these young people to marry are relatives, Samuels explains, so he plans to send his daughter Diana, 21, and later his other daughter Kazna, 19, and his son

Sammy, 16, to live with relatives in Israel, the UK, or the States. There he hopes they will wed and procreate. And then, he hopes, they and their families will return.

Help might also come if the country continues to open up to foreign investment. The logic is that with a more open business environment, some of the émigré Jews might be willing to come back. Although human rights activists urge against foreign investment in Myanmar, development continues at an aggressive pace, as witnessed by the eighteen foreign hotels under construction in the capital.

But for the moment, Samuels, thin and serious and dressed in a Burmese longyi sarong and a short-sleeved batik shirt, relies on the kindness of strangers. Visiting Jews drop a few dollars into the collection box, and richer philanthropists have helped to refurbish the white-tiled sanctuary where the Torahs are kept.

Of more immediate concern to Samuels, who inherited the role of caretaker from his father Isaac who died in 1978, is the possibility that the government will raze the Jewish cemetery, where some seven hundred people are buried. Like neighboring Chinese, Bahai'i, Moslem, Parsi, and Armenian cemeteries, the palm-tree lined Jewish graveyard lies on prime commercial land in the center of rapidly expanding Yangon. The government owns the cemetery land, as it does the land on which the synagogue stands.

Near the end of my visit to Yangon, someone calls to me as I walk down a market street. It is Rashid, my friend from the guest house.

"Did you find Moses?" he asks, a bit breathless after having run across the street. Rashid listens closely to my tale and nods. "I was just in the mosque," he explains. "I said a prayer for both of you."

I'm touched. Nobody has prayed for me for a while, at least not that I know of. I certainly don't mind. And Samuels, I'm sure, could use a bit of help.

ASIAN SYNAGOGUES, KING SOLOMON, AND THE SPICE TRADE

MYANMAR IS NOT THE ONLY COUNTRY IN THE Indian subcontinent with a synagogue. There is a synagogue in Karachi, Pakistan. And there are thirty-three synagogues in India dating from the mid-sixteenth- through the mid-twentieth century. Although many no longer function as such and today vary in their levels of preservation, several synagogues are active – most well known is the Paradesi synagogue in Jew Town, Kochi, constructed in 1568.

Today they seem like crypto-synagogues – curious Jewish places of worship in unexpected places. Yet the synagogues are symbols of what was once an active Jewish mercantile trade between the Middle East and India.

While historians know well how Islam was first brought to India by merchants and traders from the Middle East in the seventh century, only recently is evidence being uncovered illustrating that Jewish traders plied similar trade routes more than a millennia earlier.

First, there are linguistic clues.

Historian Shalva Weil of Israel's Hebrew University notes that the Bible's Book of Kings tells that King Solomon's ships, as early as 900 B.C.E., transported cargo such as *kofin* (apes), *tukim* (peacocks), and *almag* (sandalwood) to the Temple. These unique words in Hebrew, she points out, are of South Indian origin. Also, in the Book of Esther it is mentioned that the kingdom of King Ahaseuerus stretched from Hoddu, generally accepted to be India, to Kush, generally accepted to be Nubia or Ethiopia.

In 2006 archeologists discovered what they believe is the legendary port of Muziris in Kerala – mentioned by the Romans and in Tamil texts – an important, and up to now, legendary port where mercantile Jews traded in spices, pharmaceuticals, textiles, gold, silver, and silks.

Weil also notes that a fictional character named Abraham Ben Yiju, who is the narrator in Amitav Ghosh's novel *In an Ancient Land*, was, in fact, a real person. She notes that some eighty medieval documents have been found mentioning how Ben Yiju and his family traded pepper, cardamom, perfume, betel nut, and precious metals.

Doors remain shut in the quest
for this obstacle-removing god.

THE ELUSIVE
GANESHETTES

Ganesha, who removes obstacles,
isn't helping much in this particular quest.

MANDALAY

 seek protection. I seek removal of obstacles. I seek good luck.

I turn to Ganesha for help.

But he isn't listening to my ongoing quest, which is to find the origin of the ten female Ganeshas in my collection.

Ganesha, the elephant-headed son of Hindu superstar gods Shiva and Parvati, isn't the most powerful god in the Hindu pantheon. But he is easily the most popular, and every new endeavor, ranging from starting a business to sitting for an exam to courting a girl, involves invoking the pot-bellied god's blessing. He is so efficient as a door-opener that Hindu faithful pray to him before they begin their prayers to other, more portentous gods, in order that their requests will get on a fast track to the cosmos.

Ganesha is the Hindu snowplow, clearing a way for people stuck on a crowded and indifferent planet. As Gita Mehta, author of *Eternal Ganesha* puts it, "he is the Pitcher of Prosperity, the Remover of Obstacles, the Grantor of Boons, the Guarantor of Success, and the Lord of Beginnings." Sort of an Alice's Restaurant kind of deity.

However, I exaggerate. I'm not a Hindu. I don't worship Ganesha. (In fact, I have little patience for all organized religions, but I am fascinated by the dynamics that encourage people to believe in such methods of social management.) But I like him an awful lot – I like the way artists throughout South and Southeast Asia exuberantly create his images. I like his penchant for sweets. I like the (usually) cute mouse that is his vehicle. I like the idea of Ganesha and have perhaps a hundred Ganesha images in my collection.

Many of these statues, amulets, and paintings are, let's say, a bit arcane. There's a red-skinned Ganesha from Thailand in blue pantaloons, flexing his biceps like Hulk Hogan. A Javanese Ganesha in what looks like a "hunting" pose, brandishing a clearly dead deer. Indian Ganeshi in fearsome poses spearing (with dad's trident) a variety of demons, some looking like women, some like pig-snouted trolls. A Ganesha from the Indian pilgrimage town of Haridwar sailing in a dinghy, with the Sanskrit word Om emblazoned on the sail. Ganeshi in the form of the hermit sage the Thais call Phra Reussi, a variation of the Indian rishi, with flowing robes and a cute pointed hat. A Ganesha from Sri Lanka sitting in a chariot being pulled by a sturdy mouse. Rare forms of Ganeshi in which his traditional vehicle has been shifted from a mouse to a lion or pig. Thai amulets with Ganesha on one side and the goofy-faced, Khmer-origin, Phra Op-A-Kut on the other. A bone Ganesha from Nepal where Ganesha is striding purposefully, wearing flowing robes, reminding me of Buddha or Jesus. And so many more – come to my house and see my collection.

But the Ganeshi that intrigue me most are ten female Ganeshi I call Ganeshettes. For years I've been trying to find out what they are, who made them, and why.

I know only a few things with certainty.

These female Ganeshi are rare – friends in India, Thailand, Sri Lanka, Nepal, and other Ganesha-rich countries have never seen anything like these statues. I've read academic texts and checked with art gallery owners, with no enlightenment. Even experts in Hindu iconography and Burmese art, including scholars at the British Museum and SOAS, haven't a clue.

They are beautiful – clearly feminine (and most are naked), with breasts, wide hips, and long flowing hair. Some are bronze, about 30–40 cm high, of good workmanship and patina. Some are made of lesser-grade bronze and are smaller and more rustic. A couple of the statues are half a meter tall, carved from wood with wormholes. Only the wooden Ganeshettes wear clothes. Most of them are kneeling, as if in supplication. All of them look like they come from the same artistic school.

They all come from Myanmar.

And they might not be Ganeshi at all, since they don't have any of the traditional Ganesha attributes – no crown, sampot (pantaloon), trident, mouse, sweets. Some, not all, have tusks, and some of those have what looks like one broken tusk. Many of them have lotus-like devices, which could indicate more of a Buddhist origin.

So, what are they?

There is a school of Ganesha worship that reveres a female form of Ganesha called Vainayaki. But this is an ancient and esoteric precursor to modern Hindu icono-graphy, and statues of Vainayaki have been found only in India and are old, archaic, and rare.

I asked Samuel, one of my Ganesha-pushers in Rangoon (he sold me my first Ganeshette some ten years ago), what he thinks the statue represents.

Samuel, a retired dentist, suggested that the Gane-shette is really a representation of Sula Thubuddar, the junior wife of Buddha as elephant-king Saddan. The story, known to all Burmese, is a parable on mistaken hurt/anger, the problem of jumping to conclusions, and the foolish-ness of carrying a grudge (at least that's the way I interpret it.)

Here's the tale. Buddha, as Saddan, gave each of his two wives some flowers. The bouquet he gave Sula Thu-buddar (his second wife) inadvertently contained wasps or red ants. Being a suspicious and insecure woman (attri-butes I understand apply to many "junior" wives), Sula Thubuddar thought that Saddan had given her the insect-laden flowers deliberately as a sign that he loved his senior wife more than he loved her. Sula Thubuddar died of a broken heart and was reincarnated as a lovely woman who became queen to the king of Benares. She wanted revenge and insisted her human husband order a hunter to cut off Saddan's tusk (shades of Salome). But Saddan explained to the hunter that "sure, you can have my tusk, but tell Sula Thubuddar that she's wrong; I never intended to hurt her, and I love her just as much as Wife Number One." On his return to the palace, the hunter gave Sula Thubuddar the elephant-king's tusk as she had commanded, and explained Saddan's version of events. On hearing the truth (for she knew that Saddan would never lie), Sula Thubuddar fell into a regal swoon and subsequently died (again) of a broken heart.

Another friend speculated that the Ganeshettes are examples of "local genius inspired by recreational chemicals." That's as good an explanation as any, I suppose.

The first Ganeshette I bought, for about $40, is a lovely bronze statue about 30 cm high, in which the figure holds what could be lotus leaves with her arms at an angle that reminds me of a female Olympic ski competitor waving to family back home. The statue isn't new – it has a nice patina. I'd guess the age at fifty years or more.

When I bought it some twelve years ago, I asked Samuel where it came from.

At that time he simply said it was from "around Bagan."

I've kept in touch with Samuel over the years. During a recent visit to Yangon, he opened up and explained that he got it from a rural (Buddhist) temple in the hinterlands of Bagan; Samuel said the aging abbot didn't remember who had given it to the temple.

Samuel has promised to take me to the temple from where the Ganesha comes. Like a lot of Myanmar's antique dealers, Samuel gets antiques from temples and villages by supporting development projects like building water systems, toilets, and schools; by offering generators; and by giving merit-making cash contributions to the local monastery. It will be a tiring, dusty journey by car, then by bullock cart, which is just my kind of trip.

Another dealer in Bagan told me the two Ganeshettes he sold me had been in his father's collection for more than a hundred years. He had no idea where they came from.

Zaw Zaw, the Ganesha-pusher from whom I bought several statues, is part of an extended family that has antique shops in Mandalay and Pyin Oo Lin. All the shops have variations on the Ganeshettes; he and his family have clearly cornered the market on them, and I am no doubt his best customer for these curious objects.

Zaw Zaw first swore that the Ganeshettes came from Namsan, south of Lashio in Shan State, near the border with China. Then, on a subsequent visit, he swore the Ganeshettes came from Hakkar, in Chin State. I persisted. "Are you sure?"

"Of course. Really sure."

"Can you take me there?"

Zaw Zaw was reluctant. I convinced him I wasn't an antique dealer and wasn't interested in stealing his source of tribal treasures. I explained the nature of my quest. He probably thought I was a bit mad. After I promised to pay for petrol and expenses, he agreed to take me there.

I told Zaw Zaw I needed a permit to go to that part of Chin State and explained that my travel agent in Yangon would be in touch to sort out the details.

My travel agent couldn't get a straight answer out of Zaw Zaw. Neither could I, and whenever I called he was "unavailable" or "out of town." I went to his shop in late 2013 and he was "somewhere else." I called his cousin, who manages the family hotel and antique shop in Pyin Oo Lin, who said that Zaw Zaw was in jail – the family is Muslim and it seems he got involved in the Buddhist-Muslim conflicts that have rocked Myanmar. After I heard that, I went back to the (closed) shop and asked some neighbors, who corroborated the story. Zaw Zaw, a Muslim, was in jail. His cousin seemed sympathetic. I told her I knew the family was dealing with bigger issues than that of the fact that her unfortunate cousin misled a foreigner, but was there anything she could do? She made sympathetic noises and promised to follow up. As we say in the West, "the check's in the mail."

So, will I ever find the source of my Ganeshettes? Is there a village of rogue Ganeshette worshippers some-where in the Burmese hinterland? Are the statues repre-sentative of a new religious cult, or were they made by a bored genius artisan in some village workshop outside Bagan? I'll figure it out eventually, or maybe I won't. For the moment, my dozens of Ganeshas, elegant and quirky, expensive and cheap, aren't removing too many obstacles to assist me in this quest.

What I do know is that my travel agent in Yangon is typically Buddhist about the fate of my Ganesha-pusher Zaw Zaw in Mandalay. "He lied to you," my friend said. "And he's being punished." Sounds like Zaw Zaw could use a good Ganesha of his own.

A STAR IS BORN

THE PARADOX IS THAT WHILE GANESHA IS the populist god, he does not have a starring role in the major Hindu epics. Sure, countless legends have been written about the guy (there must be several dozen tales of how he got his elephant head), yet he only features in one major Cecil B. DeMille-like epic – the Mahabharata – and then only as the scribe of the mammoth saga that provides the foundation for Hindu philosophy and worldview. And Ganesha wouldn't even have that role were it not for the efforts of Hindu public relations experts, according to some social historians (well, to Jeff McNeely and me, primarily. We offered this analysis in our book *Soul of the Tiger*, and no one has told us we're wrong.). Hinduism, with its complicated and inaccessible deities was struggling in getting a foothold in largely animistic rural areas. The Hindu MadMen of the time usurped a popular animistic elephant spirit, gave him linkage with Big Time God Indra's white elephant steed Airavata, and wrote a back-story making Ganesha the son of Shiva and Parvati – a Hindu power couple of the first magnitude. But Ganesha came too late for him to be written in either the Ramayana or the Mahabharata, so the Hindu spin doctors invented a tale in which the sage Vyasa told Ganesha, "I'm going to dictate the Mahabharata; you are the designated scribe." Ganesha agreed on the condition that Vyasa never stop his recitation (quite a feat for a poem that runs some 1.8 million words in total, roughly ten times the length of the Iliad and the Odyssey combined, and more than twice the length of the Old and New Testaments of the Bible – but it's a quick read compared to the four million words of the 2013 U.S. tax code and the 11.5 million words of Obama-care regulations). During the lengthy dictation Ganesha broke his pen, and not wanting to stop the flow of the story, he broke off one of his tusks, dipped it in ink, and carried on.

Minor miracles from a tiny darkroom.

WORLD'S SMALLEST PHOTO LAB
"USES ONLY MAN ABILITY"

*Myanmar photographer has achieved success
by realizing that size matters.*

BAGAN

 Sein Win claims that his packing crate, about the size of a kitchen stove, is the "world's smallest photo lab."

The elfin photographer, 64, is not shy about advertising. Handmade signs and photocopied magazine articles in Dutch, Greek, French, Hebrew, Slovenian, and English promise visitors to Shwezigon pagoda in Myanmar's ancient city of Bagan that U Sein Win's minuscule darkroom "prints fast, in 3 minuts [sic] really." Not only is it "famous over the world," but it "uses only man ability."

Some thirty-five years ago, with a degree in geology and chemistry from Mandalay University, U Sein Win got tired of teaching chemistry, physics, and math in high school and established one of the country's first photofinishing shops. Some businesses grow into empires; U Sein Win's has shrunken to Lilliputian dimensions.

My wife and I pose for U Sein Win. With his heavy black eyeglasses tipped at a rakish angle, he crouches in front of us, clicking his decades-old Olympus Pen EE-2, a famously reliable camera that has two huge advantages for the Burmese photographer – it takes half-frame photos, meaning he can get seventy-two pictures from a single roll, and most important, he can easily open the back and cut out the exposed film for processing and reinsert the unexposed film to get ready for the next customer. As he takes a few happy snaps, his green-checked longyi falls open and three young boys make fun of the old man who is so engaged in his art that he embarrasses foreigners by his lack of modesty.

I peer into his studio. It's only as high as his waist and as deep as his arm, but somehow U Sein Win squeezes inside, creating a new profession of contortionist-photographer. It's tiny, but there is still room in the box for a poster of a sexy girl promoting Tiger Beer, an empty tube of Mr. Potato chips, a red light, and a few trays of tired chemicals that have given birth to prints of the occasional tourist's awkward smile.

It's not easy being a small businessman in today's Myanmar. Tourists are scarce – many foreigners are unsure whether a visit to Myanmar would support the military government or send a refreshing signal of solidarity to the common folk.

Visitors find much to appreciate in this vast country, longer north to south than the distance from Chiang Mai to Singapore, with ecosystems ranging from coral reefs to

Himalayan snow-covered peaks. In a Texas-sized land area almost three times the size of the UK, Myanmar has more than twice as many people as Malaysia, and those fifty million people comprise more than one hundred distinct ethnic groups.

We wander through Shwezigon, one of the more dramatic of Bagan's three thousand pagodas that lie scattered over an area two-thirds the size of Manhattan. When we return twenty minutes later, U Sein Win hands us five washed-out prints – almost monochromatic, as if they have been sitting in the sun for too long. With a marking pen he has written, "lovely couples at Bagan."

The photos cost U.S. 30 cents each. We ask him to sign his autograph and buy them all.

Respect the *nats*, or else.

❦

WATCH WHAT YOU SAY
IN MYANMAR'S SACRED FORESTS

What's a more powerful conservation incentive –
a government jail or a spiritual punishment?

ZEE-O THIT-HLA

yint Naing has one of the easier jobs in the Myanmar forestry department. Since 1999 his task has been to protect the Zee-O Thit-Hla sacred forest, which has been a government forest reserve since 1988. No one has cut a tree during that period. Is it the fear of a three-year prison sentence that has kept this cool holy grove intact while its surroundings lie barren and baking? Or is its environmental integrity due to something mystical, something far beyond government control?

While the Zee-O Thit-Hla sacred forest might have government protection, I sense that its real power, and hence the reason it survives, lies in things that go bump in the night. Throughout Asia one hears stories. A jealous wife puts a black magic curse on her husband's mistress that makes the woman go mad. A man coughs blood, and when doctors X-ray his lungs they find dozens of metal pins, put there by a sorcerer. A farmer spends the night in the forest and when dawn comes, villagers find that he has entranced a man-eating tiger into a cage.

Trouble is, it's awfully hard to actually meet some of these magic-imbued people – these surreal episodes always seem to take place in Brigadoon-like magical localities, "in a distant village, over the next hill."

When I ask what trouble could befall someone who violates the sanctity of this sacred forest in Myanmar, I expect the usual generalizations – "you'll fall sick," or "bad things will happen." So I listen with skepticism when I hear that a farmer's house had burned down after he and a companion cursed and acted disrespectfully in this holy grove outside Bagan. I figure it for just another Asian tale, an urban legend told by cosmopolitan cynics about credulous rural folks who live far from the sophisticated capitals of Bangkok, Jakarta, and Manila. Such stories are common, but irritatingly hard to analyze – one would welcome a team of Mythbusters to put some scientific empiricism into reports about men who sell their children's souls, enabling them to turn into were-pigs to get rich. Soldiers whose sacred amulets have enabled them to survive being shot. Men who magically "teleport" themselves from one point to another. People who eat glass. Even a car repair method that relies on incantations and prayers instead of mallets and soldering irons. My amateur attempts at busting these myths usually results in a stalemate due to too many degrees of separation – the person I'm talking with heard it from his sister-in-law who heard it from someone in the pub, that kind of thing. So when I was told that the people who were punished for intruding on the sacred forest in this forgotten corner of Myanmar actually existed, I was skeptical.

"No, they're real," the village elder insists. "The unfortunate men were U Aung Khin and his son-in-law U Aye San. Want to meet them?"

TO GET TO THE ZEE-O THIT-HLA FOREST (THE NAME roughly translates as "beautiful old forest of Zee O village"), I drive about ten kilometers outside the famous ruins of Bagan in the direction of Mount Popa, turn north, and bounce along for twelve kilometers on a rutted dusty track best suited for ox carts or sturdy four-wheel-drive vehicles. I pass fields of parched earth the reddish-color of a fair-skinned European after a day in the sun, a desiccated land punctuated by fallow groundnut cultivations, and one or two villages in which life in the thatched-roof houses probably hasn't changed all that much since the monumental stupas of Bagan were built a thousand years ago.

U Thu Taw, an age-softened man wearing an immaculate long-sleeved white shirt with a Nehru collar, white turban, and checked longyi in the calm manner of many Burmese, doesn't seem especially surprised to see a stranger pop into his dusty village of a thousand people and start asking about the local sacred forest.

IF A VISITOR ASKS THE RIGHT QUESTIONS HE CAN FIND sacred forests throughout the swath of Hindu/Buddhist countries that runs from India through southern China and across to Vietnam. Holy groves are protected areas that generally have no government status, but nevertheless remain forested oases in often heavily populated areas. Local people generally insist that anyone who enters these holy forests must follow strict folk taboos – no swearing or loud noise, no lewd behavior (one couple reportedly became barren after they had a tryst in the Zee-O Thit-Hla forest), and don't take anything out, not even a twig.

"Forests have guardian spirits," notes Sein Tu, retired professor of psychology of Mandalay University. "Where the spirits feel slighted by infractions such as foul language, they are believed to mete out terrible punishments to the wrongdoer, as in the case of a young man known to me who scornfully urinated in front of a nat-altar and suffered a complete mental breakdown."

AT THE ENTRANCE TO THE 40-ACRE ZEE-O THIT-HLA sacred forest, I ask if I should remove my shoes. U Thu Taw murmurs a vague incantation to the forest spirits: "This is a visitor with tender soles, give him permission to wear shoes." Apparently he receives an okay, and he nods agreement. Not wishing to tempt fate, though, I remove my hiking boots and socks.

An open-air tin-roofed shed some thirty meters into the forest contains puppet-sized statues of the forest's guardian *nat* spirits, omnipresent demi-deities that in Myanmar control important events in people's lives. Small statues of the resident *nats* welcome visitors – U Hla Tin Aung and Daw Pun Nya Yin, *nat* brother and sister, wear red robes, their hands painted golden. They extend their palms in greeting.

The air is cool inside the forest, a welcome relief from the arid, cactus-dotted landscapes outside the perimeter. I stroll amidst mature trees so large I can't put my arms around them, including several fine ficus trees, which are seldom found in the arid zone. Some thirty-five tree species have been catalogued in this oasis of green. Is Zee-O Thit-Hla a relict forest, the last example of a richer flora that existed, some experts speculate, prior to the eleventh- to thirteenth-century construction of the great temples of Bagan?

THIS IS CONSERVATION BY THE PEOPLE, FOR THE PEOPLE. Sacred groves, or "life reserves" as one villager describes them, survive today because they serve people's physical and spiritual needs.

In one sense, sacred forests fit my Cartesian, left-brained worldview – they act as watersheds, offer shelter for animals, are repositories for medicinal plants and, in an emergency and given the proper ceremonies, can provide timber to rebuild a village ravaged by fire.

But they are also places of magic. When I was a boy I

believed in gardens filled with unicorns and sprites and goblins. I know these special places existed – I saw them in my picture books and in my mind's eye.

BACK IN THE VILLAGE, I AM FINALLY INTRODUCED TO U Aye San, the man who allegedly broke the taboos concerning this sacred grove and suffered as a result. He is a middle-aged man who appears perfectly, well, normal. "My father-in-law, U Aung Khin, was acting eccentric the morning that we entered the sacred forest," U Aye San says. "Yes, we were disrespectful, but we didn't know we were breaking the taboo."

As any cop will tell you, ignorance is no excuse for breaking the law, and the spirit-policemen of Zee-O Thit-Hla Forest served punishment. "A few hours after we returned to the village, I heard a commotion," U Aye San explains. "U Aung Khin's house was burning. He was inside and got burned. But it was very odd. The cooking fire had been extinguished. The fire apparently started spontaneously, among the dried toddy palm leaves."

I am introduced to the hapless father-in-law. U Aung Khin is 84 ("my secret of long life is rice and toddy") and half deaf. Our translator shouts into his good ear but to no avail. He is either embarrassed to speak about the event, or his memory is gone. He cannot confirm or deny U Aye San's story.

On departure, I ask Myint Naing, the Zee-O Thit-Hla forest guard, which is a stronger deterrent to villagers

– the *nats* or the government. "The *nats*," he says without hesitation. "Definitely the *nats*."

Hit toward Daung Kalat and
hope the *nats* lend a helping hand.

GOLF THAT GOES
BUMP IN THE NIGHT

Nat spirits, hermit monks, and a farm boy who plays off eight make Mount Popa Golf Course an other-worldly experience.

MOUNT POPA

 here is strange magic in the air.

For a start, U Moe Ting, my caddie at this unprepossessing course in central Myanmar, tells me to "hit towards the trees."

There is no fairway in sight, just an ox cart trundling in the brush along the spot where my drive would probably land. But never mind – farm boy U Moe Ting plays off eight, using pre-WWII golf clubs, so who was I to challenge his judgment?

And he was right. I hit my drive on the second hole and the ball landed in a hidden flat patch that revealed an opening to the previously camouflaged dogleg. Local knowledge helps, especially when the *nats* are out and about.

NATS ARE THE MYSTICAL AND MISCHIEVOUS SOULS OF legendary people (who seem to have died mostly horrible deaths). They hold dominion over a place, person, or field of experience. In predominantly Buddhist Myanmar, *nats* take on the role of elves, leprechauns, Santa Claus, and kitchen gods. Lord Buddha takes care of the big things – life, death, and salvation – but *nats*, a form of animistic spirit-guardians, are where the spiritual rubber meets the road, the cosmic adjudicators of school exams and teenage romance, business success, and lottery tickets.

And Mount Popa, sometimes described as the Mount Olympus of Myanmar, is *nat* Ground-Zero. Located some fifty kilometers southeast of Bagan, this is among Myanmar's spaciest locations. Besides the ubiquitous nat-spirits, Mount Popa is home to snake charmers who control when the monsoons will arrive, a hermit cave-dwelling monk, a jungle path with so many butterflies that I felt like I was in a Lepidoptera ticker-tape parade, and a conjurer who smashed my watch with a hammer and, for a small fee, put it back together again.

A FEW DAYS AFTER MY GOLF GAME, I TREKKED AN HOUR UP a butterfly-enhanced forest path on Mount Popa, arguably the most mystical hill in this most mystical of countries, to visit a hermit monk named Venerable U Sumana.

Hesitantly, I approached the cave and saw a young

monk preparing a fire. I asked if I was disturbing him. Popping in unannounced suddenly seemed like a stupid idea – the last thing I wanted to do was get in the way of his accumulation of karma points. Nevertheless, for a recluse, U Sumana was remarkably outgoing. He had finished his morning prayers, he explained, and invited me to sit on the ledge and chat.

Several years earlier, U Sumana had taken over the cave that had been the home of U Jermani, a legendary monk who meditated in this damp, isolated ledge for fifty years. U Sumana had few possessions, few clothes, and his diet consisted of rice and vegetables. To me such isolation, deprivation, and rigor would be purgatory. I like my diversions too much – Beethoven, a fine wine, golf, pizza, and the company of friends. U Sumana, though, had a different view of his adopted home. "It's shady and cool. It's easy to get water. I'm in the middle of nature and there's no one around to distract me from my prayers." He had bright eyes and an easy smile. He explained he had seen this cave in a dream and journeyed here from distant Mon state.

My rational, Cartesian mind was racing. "But what do you do all day?" I asked.

Venerable U Sumana, 30, explained simply: "I meditate." Sometimes sitting. Sometimes moving. He showed me his walking meditation. Very, very slowly, I try to replicate his movement – I roll from my heel to the toe and hold the opposite foot in the air before placing it down. I concentrate on the action. He explains that this type of practice, called *zingyan shouk chin*, will clear my mind, help me to develop patience and acceptance. Useful, no doubt, on the course.

FROM EACH HOLE ON THE MOUNT POPA GOLF COURSE, I could see the dramatic cylindrical Daung Kalat, a volcanic plug rising 737 meters from the flat, hot plain. (Nomenclature is a bit confusing, since photogenic Daung Kalat is generally referred to as Mount Popa, but in fact is a prominent and picturesque outcrop that sits on the southwest flank of Mount Popa, which at 1,518 meters is considerably higher.) Daung Kalat is said to be the core of an extinct volcano last active twenty-five hundred years ago, and the ground around the course is strewn with pieces of petrified wood.

THE FIRST TIME I PLAYED MOUNT POPA, IN 1993, THE course was in poor shape, with subtropical scrub growing rampant on the fairways and tee boxes made of concrete-hard dirt. The holes had rarely been moved from one point on the green to another, and as a result, due to regular rain and the footsteps of golfers, the area around the holes became a meter-diameter funnel, sort of like a drain to help balls reach the target.

In the late 1990s the Mount Popa Golf Course was refurbished. The greens have been improved, but they are still tough to play because of their shape – mostly convex, like overturned saucers – so it's difficult to keep the ball on the green without it running off.

Wisely, the people who fixed up the course kept one quirky feature – the sand green on the par-four fifth hole.

This was the first time I had played on a sand green. My approach shot landed with a satisfying plop. The caddie lifted my ball, raked a path to the hole, and replaced my ball. I babied the putt and it went, oh, twenty centimeters. Finally, realizing what I had to do, I rammed a stroke of polo-like strength and the ball traveled all of one meter.

THE MOST DARING SNAKE CHARMER IN THE WORLD practices her skill in a Mount Popa cave. On the chosen morning the farmer's wife, not quite a snake priestess but more like a snake intermediary, leads a long, slow procession of villagers up the steep slopes of Mount Popa. Her neck and arms are dusted white with rice powder, she wears a loose-fitting muslin shirt over her faded sarong, she has said her prayers to the gods, and her soul has been blessed by the local Buddhist abbot. She has been given the assignment to beseech the Naga, the snake-god found throughout the subcontinent, to expedite the monsoon rains.

Approaching the shallow cave where a king cobra is lurking, she moves slowly and respectfully, murmuring apologies for disturbing the snake-god's rest. She kneels in front of the reptile and touches her forehead to the ground three times, as the snake rears up and spreads its hood in alarm. The priestess serenely rises and undulates in slow, sensuous rhythms, using her body like a snake charmer's flute.

After several minutes of her trance-like dance, the priestess induces the cobra to strike. But the direction of the strike is predictable, and the woman steps back so that the cobra's fangs, ejaculating a teaspoonful of deadly venom, hit only her loose robe. The dance continues. The cobra strikes again and again, but the amount of venom that drips down the front of the woman's robe lessens with each strike. After five minutes the snake is thoroughly confused, weary, and frustrated, and exhausted of venom.

The cobra's head is still reared a meter off the ground, and the woman gives the snake three quick kisses on top of its head. Bowing low, she murmurs her thanks to the Lord Naga and backs away slowly, as a commoner always takes leave of a king. The crowd, their tension relieved at last, follows the woman back down the mountain, small boys laughing and kicking up dust and villagers chatting. To the southwest, distant storm clouds gather over the Gulf of Martaban, soon to release their life-giving liquid to the parched rice fields below.

IN THIS LAND WHERE GOOD FORTUNE COMES FROM surprising sources, the Mount Popa caddies invariably bring good luck. On one tree-lined hole, U Moe Ting stationed himself out of sight of the tee, halfway down the fairway, acting as fore-caddie to watch the flight of the ball in the (not unreasonable) expectation that I would hit an errant drive. I was certain that I sliced my ball into the forest, but when I arrived, U Moe Ting greeted me with "good news, sir" and proudly pointed out my ball, which was not only sitting on the fairway, but residing quite comfortably on a rare tuft of grass.

I felt that magic like that should be rewarded, and I left U Moe Ting my glove and half a dozen balls.

CRYPTO-GOLF

I'm intrigued by Myanmar's seldom-visited golf courses, a British legacy that survives in unusual places. For me this is crypto-golf – golf where it oughtn't be. Some of the highlights of my ongoing quest to play all these isolated courses follow.

It was a rainy weekday in December, with southern Myanmar receiving the tail end of Typhoon Durian that had swept through Southeast Asia, when I appeared at the Kawthaung Golf Club and asked for a game. The manager, U Naing Htay, reluctantly agreed to brave the elements and accompany me, later telling me that I was the first foreigner to grace his attractive course.

Whether or not this is true (and I have my

doubts), the point is that good golf, at a refreshingly low price and in friendly company, can be found throughout Myanmar.

The Texas-sized country of forty-seven million people, which had a British colonial past, has one hundred and two courses according to Duncan Weir, director of golf development at the Royal and Ancient, a group based in Scotland that promotes golf worldwide. Eleven of these courses have opened since 1990, Weir says, and some sixty thousand people in the country play the game.

Some of these courses are of international standard, such as the Gary Player-designed Pun Hlaing Golf Club in Yangon, the country's largest city, and up until recently, its capital.

But I became intrigued by the large number of isolated, quirky, smaller courses sprinkled throughout the country, ruled by a military junta not known for its sense of humor or pursuit of aimless pleasure. This, for me, is classic crypto-golf – golf where it oughtn't be. And since only seven hundred fifty thousand tourists visit annually, a visitor has a pretty good chance of getting a tee time.

On many of these "distant greens," grass was a bit bare or shaggy, the fairways too rectangular, the bunkers overgrown, the greens made of sand (locally called "browns"), and the golf clubs I was offered sometimes resembled garden implements more than the expensive clubs I have at home. But then I reminded myself that I was playing on empty courses, paying less than a dollar in green fees, and, if U Naing Htay at Kawthaung was right, breaking new ground.

In Katha, where George Orwell wrote *Burmese Days*, a golf course meanders through a teak forest, and if you're lucky you will get an extra bounce by hitting one of the two concrete helicopter landing pads on the first fairway.

Myitkyina, in northern Myanmar near the Chinese border, boasts two golf courses. Soe Myint, the manager of the nine-hole Myitkina Golf Club, took special pride in pointing out one of the course's more diabolical design features, which I found on several courses – elevated greens shaped like upturned saucers.

And in Mawlaik, on the Chindwin River and accessible only by river, Scottish teak planters built a nine-hole course in 1936 with two sand greens. Members proudly say it's the oldest (or second oldest or third oldest, no one is quite sure) course in the country. Local rules allow a free drop if your ball lands in the droppings of a wandering water buffalo.

A relict typewriter from Orwell's epoch
still works well for administrators in Katha.

SEARCHING FOR ORWELL

A backwater town in Upper Myanmar was the site for Orwell's
Burmese Days, *a book that takes no prisoners.*

KATHA

here are worse travel strategies than to visit places with evocative names.

There's Timbuktu, Congo, and Okavango in Africa; Salvador de Bahia, Darien, and Patagonia in Latin America, names that purr with history and poetry.

But Asia's resonant place names beckon to me above all others. There's Sumatra, Java, and Borneo; Malacca, Vientiane, and Makassar; Kelantan, Kathmandu, and Ayudhya. Not to mention the rivers: Ganges and Yangtze, Mahakam and Mekong. And the one I was headed toward: Ayeyarwaddy.

My destination was Katha, a small town on the Ayeyarwaddy (Irrawaddy) River, which has achieved a modicum of recognition. It was here, between 1926 and 1927, that a British policeman named Eric Blair spent six months as one of ninety British police officers in Burma. Eric Blair, who subsequently took the pen name George

Orwell, based his 1934 novel *Burmese Days* on a fictionalized version of Katha that he dubbed Kyauktada (which is derived from the name of a district in Yangon).

I STARTED MY JOURNEY BY FLYING TO THE NORTHERN town of Myitkyina, then driving six hours to the river town of Bhamo where I boarded a "speedboat," a sixty-passenger vessel ten meters wide and some forty meters long, for the six-hour journey downriver to Katha.

The arrival of the boat in Katha is one of the high points of the day for small traders, porters, and trishaw drivers, who politely (this is Myanmar, after all, not Egypt) vie for the custom of arriving travelers.

The river here is about a kilometer wide, placid, with exposed sandbanks that can hinder big boat traffic during the dry season.

There is no harbor, and visitors clamber up the dirt river bank. I was relieved to see that there wasn't a taxi in sight. Just a couple of horse carts and a handful of trishaws – not the mechanized *tuk-tuks* of Bangkok, but old-fashioned man-pedaled three-wheelers, calmly waiting in front of a large Buddhist temple.

There has been a mini tourist boom in Katha in recent years, largely comprised of folks looking for Orwell. The Ayeyarwaddy Guest House, which seems to get most of the foreign visitors, receives about two hundred travelers during the peak season, according to the owner, Soe Than Shwe. Reflecting this trend – or perhaps leading it, one never knows – the 2005 edition of the *Lonely Planet* guide, which in the edition of 2000 did not even mention Katha, currently devotes two pages to the town.

THE TOURIST BOOMLET WAS PARTLY SPURRED BY EMMA Larkin's 2004 book *Secret Histories: Finding George Orwell in a Burmese Teashop*. In her book, Larkin (a pseudonym), makes the argument that *Burmese Days* "was the beginning of Orwell's uncanny and prophetic trilogy [*Burmese Days*, *Animal Farm*, and *Nineteen Eighty-Four*] that told the history of present-day Myanmar."

Her argument goes like this:

> *Burmese Days* ... chronicles the country's period under British colonialism. Not long after Myanmar became independent from Britain in 1948, a military dictator sealed off the country from the outside world, launched 'The Burmese Way to Socialism', and turned Myanmar into one of the poorest countries in Asia. The same story is told in Orwell's *Animal Farm* ... Finally, in *Nineteen Eighty-Four*, Orwell's description of a horrifying and soulless dystopia paints a chillingly accurate picture of Myanmar today, a country ruled by one of the world's most brutal and tenacious dictatorships.

Regardless of whether her theory holds water, it is certainly intriguing; no doubt Orwell would have recognized the "Newspeak"-like mentality behind a 1989 Burmese government statement that "truth is true only within a certain period of time. What was truth once may no longer be truth."

To a casual visitor, the oppression of Myanmar's military-run State Peace and Development Council (which indeed sounds like a parody name derived from *Nineteen Eighty-Four*) is not apparent. But if people in Myanmar decide to trust you, and you give them an opening, they will first look over their shoulder to see who else might be listening, shake their heads, and say something like "we pray for a change, but what can we do?" Indeed, one young man in a teashop in Katha, much like Larkin's friends, unhesitatingly declared, not terribly *sotto voce*, that "we have no human rights, no power. All the power is held by"—here he patted his shoulder to indicate military epaulettes—"the men with the stars."

IN ONE PASSAGE LARKIN WRITES OF AN INTERVIEW WITH an elderly scholar:

> "George Orwell," I said slowly. "G-E-O-R-G-E-O-R-W-E-L-L." But the old Burmese man just kept shaking his head. We were sitting in the baking-hot front room of his house in a sleepy port town in Lower Myanmar. I was about to give up but made one final stab.
>
> "George Orwell," I repeated. 'The author of *Nineteen Eighty-Four*." The old man's eyes suddenly lit up. He looked at me with a brilliant flash of recognition, slapped his forehead gleefully, and said, "You mean the prophet!"

REGARDLESS OF THE POLITICS OF MYANMAR, KATHA IS A pleasant place to spend a few days and visit Orwell sites.

The tennis court features in *Burmese Days* as a place that most of the British characters avoided whenever possible – they were too enervated by heat and gin ("the cement of Empire," Orwell writes) to undertake any exercise. Foreign visitors to Katha several years ago wrote about the disgraceful state of the court. Today the court has been renamed the River View Tennis Club, and it boasts an all-weather surface, a new net, and local players enthusiastically working on their backhands.

About a hundred meters behind the River View Tennis Club, toward the river but not on its banks, as the book's fictional geography has it, sits the old English club, whose building and goings-on served as the model for the stubbornly all-white Kyauktada Club, the fictional focal point of *Burmese Days*. Indeed, so much of the book's action takes place in and around the Kyauktada Club that the book could easily be transformed into a stage play, with the Club serving as the main set.

Orwell decorated his fictional Kyauktada Club with "a forlorn library of five hundred mildewed novels and ... a mangy billiard table." The "unhomelike" lounge was adorned with dusty skulls of sambar deer. A frequent sound was colonial whinging when the ice ran out. It was a tatty, gin-soaked refuge for heat-rashed Brits who had little better to do than dream about "home," and remi-nisce about the good old days when one could send a misbehaving servant to the jail with a note reading,

"Please give the bearer fifteen lashes." Orwell said of the Club that "People thoroughly on each other's nerves meet night after night in a desperate effort to forget the boredom of their own existence ... The Club is not alone a place of enjoyment, it is a symbol of racial solidarity."

On the afternoon I visited the site, two part-time teachers were giving after-school tuition to young students. One teacher was writing a lesson in English verb tenses on the blackboard – "U Win (clean) his compound yesterday," while a second teacher was putting her young charges through algebra challenges.

After class the English teacher introduced himself as U Pe Aung, whose day job was manager of the agricultural cooperative that now had ownership of the building. On the large main floor, U Pe Aung gave me a tour. The teak floor was undoubtedly the same as decades past, but the walls had been stuccoed and whitewashed, and the tiled roof had been replaced by tin. On one of the seven empty desks stood an ancient Olympia typewriter, and on another rested a Gestetner 145, a stencil duplicating machine from the 1960s.

"Yes, we get quite a few visitors," U Pe Aung said. He estimated that some four thousand tourists visited Katha during the period of November through February. The number sounds high, but he said it included people who were cruising on one of the luxury live-aboard boats plying the Ayeyarwaddy, which make a quick stop in the town that Orwell made famous.

I CAN ONLY SIGHTSEE FOR SO LONG AND ASKED whether there was a golf course nearby. Soe Than Shwe, the owner of the Ayeyarwaddy Guest House, picked me up in a meticulously maintained World War II-era Willys jeep, one of the few cars in town, and took me to Katha's Ayar Shweli Golf Club. "Orwell didn't play golf," Soe Than Shwe asserted, perhaps accurately, since the game is not mentioned in Orwell's various Burmese writings.

He added, "Orwell didn't like Myanmar," a declaration shared by many of the relatively few Burmese who have actually read *Burmese Days*.

Emma Larkin heard similar criticisms and defended Orwell to one of her friends who said that Orwell was anti-Burmese: Orwell's ability, Larkin wrote:

> was able to voice what he saw as the truth no matter how painful or awkward it might be. In *Burmese Days*, Orwell was simply painting a picture of how he saw things in Myanmar. It is not that Orwell disliked Myanmar or the Burmese, I said: it was the system he disliked. He was condemning a political framework that made good men – both Burmese and British – do bad things.

Indeed, the book takes a cynical view of virtually all the virtue-challenged players. Larkin recounts the list of "repellent" characters: "Flory's Burmese mistress is sluttish and desperate, his servant is obsequious, and a corrupt Burmese magistrate attempts to scheme and blackmail his way into the British-only club," which is a key plot line in the novel.

Orwell is, refreshingly, an equal-opportunity misanthrope. The British in *Burmese Days* are desperately lonely, borderline alcoholics, backbiting, racist prigs, who mouth platitudes about bringing civilization to the savages but whose real sentiment lies closer to that of one character who raves: "No natives in this Club! We've ruined the Empire. This country's only rotten with sedition because we've been too soft with them. The only possible policy is to treat 'em like the dirt they are." The unlovable British in the book are angry to be in Upper Myanmar, bitterly realizing that they were stuck in the humid backwater because they had no home left in England.

ORWELL'S FICTIONAL KYAUKTADA HAD A POPULATION of four thousand; today's Katha has about eighty thousand. It seems a prosperous town, spread for several kilometers along the west bank of the river. Money comes in from trading in sugar cane, beans, peanuts, and timber. The markets are full and animated, and dozens of shops, many of them charming wooden buildings, sell everything from home-made cowbells to brightly packaged Chinese rice cookers and DVD players.

I would have enjoyed another day or two in Katha, but the ferry was leaving for another mellifluously named town where Blair/Orwell lived – Mandalay, some 320 kilometers to the south.

EMPIRE-BAITING

Orwell's clearest opinions about how he equally disliked the British Empire and its Burmese subjects can be seen in his 1936 essay "Shooting an Elephant."

Working as a policeman in Moulmein in southern Myanmar, Orwell was called on to deal with a domestic elephant that, while in a state of musth, had killed a coolie and destroyed shops and homes. It was a time of racial and political tension: "If a European woman went through the bazaars alone, somebody would probably spit betel juice over her dress, [while] young Buddhist priests would stand on street corners and jeer at Europeans." Orwell didn't want to kill the elephant, but the "sea of yellow faces ... expected it of me ... I was only an absurd puppet pushed to and fro ... I perceived in this moment that when the white man turns tyrant, it is his own freedom that he destroys." It became a question of pressure and face:

> A sahib has got to act like a sahib; he has got to appear resolute ... [to do nothing] was impossible. The crowd would laugh at me. And my whole life, every white man's life in the East, was one long struggle not to be laughed at.

The elephant (midway through the essay Orwell shifts the animal's descriptive pronoun from "it" to "him") takes a hideously long time to die. Three shots with an elephant gun, then more with a smaller rifle. A metaphor for the resilience of the British empire? Or for the inevitability of national independence?

POLITICALLY CORRECT ORWELL

Orwell was ahead of his time in condemning the use of what he called insulting nicknames for those of other races. He argued that it was possible to do "a little to mitigate the horrors of the colour war" by ensuring the word "native" was not used in a derogatory sense, that "Negro" was always given an initial capital letter, and by substituting "Chinese" for "Chinaman" and "Moslem" for "Mohamedan."

WRITERS WHO WILL NOT DIE

Dying of tuberculosis in the Cotswolds in 1950, Orwell ignored the advice of his doctors to take it easy and wrote three pages for a novella with the working title "A Smoking Room Story." The story, which he never completed, would have been a final gaze at Myanmar. Coughing blood, and surrounded by classic British novels and studies of Stalin and Hitler, with a bottle of rum hidden under his bed, Orwell couldn't get Myanmar out of his system. He told a friend that "a writer who has a book left in him to write will not die."

Globalization is the new reality of the rural world.

IN SEARCH OF A
"MORE VIRGIN" DESTINATION

A traveler's dream – being the first foreigner to trek in Nagaland.

LAHE

y travel agent friend in Yangon sent me an itinerary for a trek to Nagaland, with a comment every traveler dreams of: "This place is more virgin; you will be first to visit."

This was such exciting news that the anti-porn filter on the computer of a potential trekking companion blocked my incoming message transmitting this happy news, perhaps considering it overly titillating.

First foreign visitor. How often does that happen? Today every seemingly remote village appears to have been intruded upon by an assortment of tourists, adventurers, shucksters, plant collectors, missionaries, imperialists, development experts, thrill-seekers, and do-gooders. Where are the blank spots on the map with the notation "Here be dragons"?

Some two million Naga live in the Himalayan foothills

straddling India, where the majority of Naga live, and Myanmar, which is home to some one hundred thousand Naga – nobody is too sure of the precise number. Foreign, mostly British, explorers, government officials, and anthropologists have trekked up and down the corrugated hills of Indian Nagaland for over a century. Visitors are welcome in "safe" Indian Nagaland destinations, but the central government in distant Delhi doesn't want outsiders to witness too closely the ongoing Naga independence movement, with related protests about dams, environmental destruction, and land disputes, and therefore restricts access to large swathes of the region.

In spite of its important but often overlooked role in World War II, the Myanmar side is largely off the tourist and development map. An annual Naga New Year's festival featuring a giant hornbill (similar to the Iban Gawai Kenyalang festival of the Iban, a hill tribe in Sarawak in Malaysian Borneo) draws a few dozen curiosity seekers, but for the most part the visitors were not allowed to leave the towns where such celebrations were held. And then my "more virgin" friend Saw Hla Chit said he could obtain permits for us to trek through, and spend the night in, isolated Naga villages along the upper Chindwin River.

MODERN TRAVEL MAPS OF MYANMAR, LIKE MY 1:1,000,000 Freytag & Berndt edition, show the Naga region as a pale green hilly area to the west of the Chindwin River, abutting the cream-colored lowlands to the east. No villages can be seen on this map, but the town of Lahe is marked.

I went to the Royal Geographical Society and British Library in London to look at old colonial maps from the nineteenth century and British War Office World War II-era maps to get a better sense of where we would be going. I came away with two impressions. The first was a renewed appreciation of British mapmakers who traipsed through isolated corners of the Earth with their surveying equipment, compasses, and altimeters, trying to make sense of our planet's geography. (Mapmaking is tough. Here's a challenge. Make a map of an area, say, radiating one kilometer from your house, an area you know well. Mark major landmarks, elevation changes, compass directions, different sized roads. Then check it against an "official" map. Bet you'll be surprised how difficult it is to make an accurate representation of reality.) The second impression was that Nagaland is a difficult place in which to travel. On these early maps large chunks of land were left blank with the notation "Unsurveyed." Sprinkled throughout were notations like "Dense bamboo forest" and "Steep forested terrain." The hills, shown in black and white relief, looked like fissures of the brain, one fold merging into another, quite beautiful to look at on a map but a pain in the neck to walk.

Obviously geography tempers culture. General-izations are tricky, but I've found that people in hill tribes throughout Asia are self-sufficient, resilient, private (but friendly enough if they trust you), and able to sit still for hours without having iPad withdrawal. They are in terrific physical shape. This is partly due to the realities of life in cold, damp places without much access to medical care or good food. It's natural selection; if you're sickly you die. It's said that one aspect of Naga beauty – for both men and women – is a leg with a shapely, well-muscled calf.

Morning clouds give their homes a mysterious aspect that suggests ghosts and demons are out and about. But the mist, and significant rainfall, also makes the farms productive, up to a point. Without the technology and regular water supply of the lowland farmers, people in the hills grow one crop of dry rice a year, instead of the two or three crops of wet rice in the more sophisticated coastal areas.

It can be a tough life. In his book *The Jacaranda Tree*, telling the story of English settlers in Myanmar traveling through Nagaland with the Japanese army in pursuit, H.E. Bates wrote:

> It had always been a country of continual exodus up there: a wandering from place to place by thin cattle, lean men, sore-eyed children, women with faces of teak-wood, an endless search for the hills' less bitter places.

He dismissed the people he met as "the eaters of opium, the headhunters, forever squatting, spitting chewed betel nut and waiting silently for nothing."

Because the hill tribes are farther from the cities, they have less access to education and communications and are forced to create their own entertainment and stories instead of relying on TV dramas. To be sure, there is a surfeit of drama in merely surviving, but getting a villager to tell stories that sound logical and detailed is a tough ask. Partly it's reticence, an innate shyness that has evolved in conjunction with trepidation about outsiders coming in and doing horrible things.

And partly it's a different way of thinking. We in the West grow up comfortable with narrative story structures. However, getting a story out of a hill tribe elder often requires repetition of the most basic type of questions: "Tell me again which came first, your dream or the day you caught the tiger?" Let's chalk some of this up to the fact that they are talking to a foreigner, and the conversation is being translated (not always accurately) through intermediaries.

Consider U Mg Nan, the shaman of Long Khin village. He has tales to tell, but I didn't succeed in learning much about him or the work he does. Physically he presents a curious sight – torn T-shirt, old green-checked longyi, droopy eyes, and a wispy moustache. But what sets him apart is that he wears a blonde wig, cut in a bob, and struts around like Johnny Depp as Captain Jack Sparrow. He offered to sell us a basket decorated with a monkey skull that he used for collecting medicinal plants. Maybe I didn't ask the right questions. Perhaps he didn't trust me. Or I simply didn't have enough time to get to know the guy. U Mg Nan, 65, had stories to tell, and I didn't get any of them.

IT WAS ALMOST DISTURBINGLY EASY TO GET TO "MORE virgin" Nagaland. Farquhar, a friend of some forty years, Saw Hla Chit, our "more virgin" travel agent, and I took an early-morning flight from Mandalay to the market town of Khamti, on the upper Chindwin River. We crossed the river on a small boat. We had been expecting to drive to the even smaller town of Lahe by public bus (which in reality was an open truck), but Saw Hla Chit managed to get use of the four-wheel-drive vehicle owned by the Naga Development Authority, and the seven-hour drive on a dirt road to Lahe was done in comfort. From Lahe we walked or took motorcycles to four villages, which, in spite of my notes and the photos, seem to merge in my memory. This is a truism of traveling, at least for me – situations that are intense at the time quickly lose their vitality as soon as I leave, wilting like a hothouse plant transplanted into a too-chilly open-air garden.

NAGALAND WITNESSED BRITISH AND JAPANESE TROOP movements during World War II. The Japanese, ensconced in Yangon, had hoped to reach Calcutta and Delhi through the Naga Hills but were pushed back by Allied forces, including troops led by crusty General Joseph (Vinegar Joe) Stilwell. On the Indian side, at Kohima, the delightfully named "Battle of the Tennis Court" came to be known as the Stalingrad of the East, where one of the most important battles of the Second World War took place. Even today a visitor can see skeletons of some of the seven hundred bridges on the 1,600-kilometer long Ledo Road – built by U.S. Army engineers to create a supply route from India to China – considered one of the greatest engineering feats of World War II.

———※———

Actually, it's not hard to be the first European (polite descriptor for a Caucasian from a rich, cosmopolitan country) to be the first person of his ilk to visit a particular place. You just have to be prepared to drive along rough roads and walk a bit, and anyone can do the same. So what?

———※———

Folks in Makyan and San Tone villages said a handful of Europeans had visited their villages some years ago, following the New Year's Festival in the nearest town of Lahe. With a new road halfway finished, no doubt these villages will become more popular.

Not much farther, but in a different direction from Lahe, people in Lone Khin and Kha Lei villages claimed we were the first foreigners to visit.

———※———

Naga villages are spread along hilltops, and the houses and agricultural fields are visible from great distances, appearing tantalizingly close but far enough away to require some effort to get there. This penchant for hilltop living comes from the Nagas' desire for security from other marauding tribes, but it makes it harder to get water. One welcome side benefit is the altitude, which at about 1,500 meters means it's not overly hot and the hills are largely mosquito-free.

Houses are mostly made of wood and thatch; mercifully, tin roofs have yet to make a significant dent on Naga architecture. Villages sprawl on steep hills. There are no paths, and while traction was fine during our dry-season visit, during the rainy season rivulets of muddy water turn the village into a pratfall opportunity, particularly for less-than-sure-footed visitors.

From the village the views are dramatic, with hills everywhere. But virgin forest, along with much of the wildlife, is long gone. The farms create a patchwork of green and brown that jumbles into the farms of adjacent villages.

The wildlife one does see comes in the form of domestic creatures – pigs roam freely as large, snorting, black-bristled beasts that can devour an unfenced garden in minutes. And every thatched-roof extended-family house features dozens of dramatic skulls of mithun – a domestic form of the gaur, also called the Indian bison – the world's largest wild cattle. Wealth is measured by the number of mithun a family owns, and major rituals are not properly consecrated without significant animal sacrifices.

MY QUEST TO VISIT THE NAGA, AND THEIR HILL TRIBE cousins worldwide, is admittedly Euro-centric, blatantly egotistical, and reveals more than a tinge of colonial adventurism. Yet the idea has always intrigued me; I fancy myself an explorer going where none have ventured before.

Is this innocent amateur anthropology or arrogant tourism-colonialism? A mature curiosity about this great big world we live in or a teenager's rebellion against the ho-hum of daily life?

Why do I travel to places like Nagaland?

On the intellectual side, I want to see how simple societies handle the transformation to cash-commerce, introduced religion, and external governance.

Sometimes, especially at dinner parties, I might suggest that I visit isolated hill tribes in order to write gritty, empathetic exposés of environmental and social injustices, leaving unsaid but implied the suggestion that my prose is as smooth as old bourbon, as sinewy as cafeteria steak.

I rationalize my quest by explaining that I'm studying tribal communities, which live relatively isolated from Western habits and consumerism. This is important because such societies are disappearing, either through genocide or, more commonly, because power brokers in the capitals hit them with a double-whammy – they steal traditional land and aggressively promote a homogenous national identity.

That's all true, but it's also a lot of politically correct hogwash. There is a lot of ego involved. I like to test myself physically, do things that my friends wouldn't. I like being hot and cold. Dusty and soggy. I like the smell of wood fires. I like sleeping on wooden floors and extricating myself at 2:00 a.m. from a sleeping bag to wander out to the scrub in back, snorting pigs watch out, to pee. I like not bathing for five days. I like walking like an exhausted zombie up one more sun-drenched hill because there isn't any alternative. Being out of range of cell phones and far from medical care. Hoarding a Snickers bar for a moment of great need.

Visiting a "more virgin" village is exactly what I enjoy. And I enjoy it partly because I'm good at it.

I like to hunker in the dust with old guys and ask about their tattoos. I like sleeping on bamboo floors, with chickens and children running about. I like taking care of my bodily functions like the proverbial bear in the woods. I like it because I can do it, because I'm still fit enough to do it, because I'm still ornery enough to be different, because I like to feel I've earned a luxury hotel bed at the end of the journey.

The Nagas, like the numerous hill tribes of Borneo, Vietnam, Laos, Sumatra, Myanmar, and Cambodia I've visited, are intriguingly "ethnic." I don't know how else to describe folks who weave intricate baskets, who rely on shamans to cure illness and dispel evil spirits, who weave blankets from dog hair, wear monkey skulls and bear fur on their straw hats, who wear, admittedly only on "dress-up" days, elaborate headgear adorned with the canine teeth of wild boar and hornbill feathers.

How superficial of me to engage in such cultural porn. But there it is.

CONSIDER THE EMOTIONALLY LOADED AND SEDUCTIVE phrase "headhunter." What images it evokes.

Until the moral and legal restrictions of the British and fundamentalist Christian missionaries came into force, both the Ibans as well as the Nagas were robust headhunters, although for different reasons. The Nagas felt that human heads ensure a good harvest (a 1911 article in the *Burma Research Society Journal* noted that "arms and legs were cut apart in the most horrifying way because [the Nagas] believed [the] longer and deeper the pain and horror was, greater the good return would be.") The Ibans in Borneo, a tribe I first encountered some forty-five years ago when I lived in the Malaysian state of Sarawak, however, took heads as part of an elaborate rite of passage. In retrospect I imagine myself at my suburban New Jersey Bar Mitzvah, standing in front of the expectant congregation and holding up a still-dripping head (perhaps of the school bully Tommy), and proudly claiming, "Today I am a man."

SINCE I WAS A CHILD I'VE BEEN INTRIGUED BY DISTANT horizons. It was armchair imagining, mostly, writing school reports about Tibet and reading *The Wonderful Flight to the Mushroom Planet*, the first book I ever read that had no pictures.

In time I graduated from boyhood dreaming to the real thing – having the means and opportunity to journey far.

When I spend time with welcoming, relatively un-Western people like the Naga, I hear of an occurrence that I not only don't understand, but in a dozen lifetimes would have no hope of comprehending.

And each day I will find someone willing to explain what's going on, with more patience probably than I would explain the rules of baseball to a first-time visitor to America.

My Cartesian, logical, scientific, fact-oriented left brain says one thing, but the smoke-and-mirrors reality in front of me says something else. There are more things in heaven and earth ..., I tell myself.

Jonathan Glancey, in *Nagaland*, describes this drive:

> There is in many of us a desire to both live a civilised life and experience, if only temporarily, a wilder, less controlled world. The tricky thing is that to do so we need to step into other people's everyday lives. And such trespasses tend to expose our dreams as just that: dreams. Nevertheless, the reality of such places, even if so very different from the stuff of our expectations, has the power to make us think differently about the "civilised" world we return to.

WHY DO BOYS LEAVE HOME AND SET OFF ON adventures?

Peter Kedit, an Iban who is former director of the Sarawak (Malaysia) Museum, might call this kind of travel a form of *berjalai* practiced by the Iban tribe, part of a young man's rite of passage in which he travels far and seeks exotic (and hopefully lucrative) experiences.

Similarly, Stanford University neuro-endocrinologist Robert Sapolsky discussed self-exile in the context of young male primates leaving the nest:

> Another key to our success [as humans] must have something to do with this primate legacy of getting an itch around adolescence. What is going on with that individual's genes, hormones, and neurotransmitters to make it hit the road? An adolescent female chimp cranes to catch a glimpse of the chimps from the next valley. New animals, a whole bunch of 'em! To hell with logic and sensible behavior, to hell with tradition and respecting your elders, to hell with this drab little town, and to hell with that knot of fear in your stomach. Curiosity, excitement, adventure – the hunger for novelty is something fundamentally daft, rash, and enriching that we share with our whole taxonomic order.

Although I'm well past adolescence, I continue my Peter Pan travels, even though my knees are wonky and my cholesterol is too high.

EVEN TODAY, IN OUR SUPPOSEDLY ENLIGHTENED WORLD, sophisticated people (the kind of folks who dislike the term "tourist" and refer to themselves as "travelers") are intrigued by esoteric customs and costumes. The government-run Sarawak Tourism Board in Malaysia, on the island of Borneo, invites visitors to spend the night with descendants of Iban headhunters; tour operators are not shy about promoting images of tribal folks wearing loincloths or vests made of clouded leopard skin and caps adorned with hornbill feathers. The dramatic and photo-genic folks a visitor sees during an Iban cultural show wave machete-like parangs while stomping about on the bamboo floor of a scenic longhouse. When I first lived in Sarawak, in 1969, many rural riverine longhouses had little sanitation. The river offered you a toilet, a place to wash your clothes and go fishing, a means to travel to another village, and water for bathing and cooking. The communal open-air bamboo terrace often was a playground for small children, dogs, and chickens, with pigs snorting below the elevated kitchens. To a middle-class boy from New Jersey it was terribly exotic, the "real" Sarawak. Today virtually all of Sarawak's longhouses boast electricity and TV, and at least rudimentary plumbing. The fancy dress is reserved for festivals. It's all very civilized. Modern-day Sarawak is a bit like Hawaii, with people showing off traditional dances and costumes when they feel like it (which sometimes means when someone is paying). The next day, be it in Sarawak or Honolulu, you're likely to meet them at the 7-Eleven or the university lecture hall.

There are, of course, distinctions between "cultural tourism" and more outrageous behavior, such as the "human safaris" organized in the Andaman Islands of India in which visitors, who are driven along a road cut through tribal territory, ogle near-naked members of the Jarawa tribe.

And there are borderline cases like the gawking tourists who visit villages in Thailand housing "long-necked" women of Myanmar's Padaung tribe. It's unseemly, it's degrading, it continues, partly because the ladies with coils of bronze around their necks allow it to continue, earning more money posing for photographs and selling trinkets than they would back on the farm.

Where possible in Nagaland we stayed in the village's "monastery," a grand name for a solid wooden house where the local Buddhist monk and often a few young novices lived. These structures were infinitely more comfortable than bunking in a village house, where we would have had to sleep next to the open fire within earshot of all the domestic noises that become irritating awfully quickly, and where we would have been woken during the night by curious dogs who stopped by to have a sniff. One evening, in Makyan, I was happily getting ready for bed and had already put on my sleeping sarong and climbed into my sleeping bag, which was placed near the altar. I was trying to read but was in that netherworld between page-turning and dreaming when people started to arrive. I stayed where I was, figuring they were coming to visit Saw Hla Chit, who was resting on the other side of the room. Then more chattering people quickly filed in, and then the monk arrived and turned on a TV with a DVD player. He played ten minutes of Burmese music videos and then started his sermon. I was in the awkward position of being in everyone's line of sight, perhaps sacrilegiously close to the Buddha statue, and the room was filled with people. I finally extricated myself from the sleeping bag and huddled back to the other end of the house. I consoled myself with the thought that while I might have been rude, I was indirectly earning merit just by being there, since we always made generous donations of cash, food, medicines, and footballs to the monks in residence.

HOW SHOULD I DESCRIBE THESE PEOPLE, WHO HAVE THEIR own language, their own customs and rituals, who consider themselves as a unified group, but who also have strong links with various government, religious, and commercial bureaucracies.

Words can unite people; they can also cause confusion. Take the terms "indigenous," "tribal," and "uncontacted."

Survival International, while noting that distinctions can be "problematic," does a good job of trying to sort out the terminology. They suggest:

> Indigenous means the same as "native," but in many places that word is not used now because it carries too many negative colonial associations ... The term "indigenous peoples" is used today to describe a group that has had ultimate control of their lands taken by later arrivals; they are subject to the domination of others.

A "tribe," according to Survival International, describes:

a distinct people, dependent on their land for their livelihood, largely self-sufficient, and not integrated into the national society ... There are an estimated one hundred and fifty million tribal individuals [in more than sixty countries], constituting around forty percent of indigenous individuals.

Although tribal land ownership rights are recognized in international law, they are not properly respected anywhere, the group says.

And then there is the almost-mythical subset of "uncontacted people."

Survival International describes "uncontacted people" as "Peoples who have no peaceful contact with anyone in the mainstream or dominant society. There are about one hundred uncontacted tribes in the world." There are two key phrases in that definition – "no peaceful contact" and "mainstream or dominant society." The Naga clearly do not fit into that rarefied description.

The Nagas I visited in Myanmar have plenty of contact with the "outside" world. The Naga districts elect five members of parliament to the federal government and receive various forms of support. The government is building roads throughout the region, a development welcomed by the Nagas. Some houses in Naga villages have solar panels and can receive television and run a few electric lights (or more annoyingly, play loud Burmese pop music on CD players). Richer men have motorcycles. Some of the children go to school in town; a very few are given scholarships by Indian Naga associations to study on the other side of the border. They buy supplies in town. They are visited by health workers and are savvy enough to sell their products to traders without getting cheated. They are rural and don't have a lot of cash, but they are hardly unknown to outsiders nor do they intend to remain in isolation. They want pretty much what people everywhere want – dignity, a share of the wealth of the nation, recognition of their tribal identity and claims to their land, a political voice, and a healthy future for their children.

AS A BONUS THE NAGA HAVE A VARIETY OF GODS TO choose from. They respect animist spirits which, refreshingly for me, imbue the air with the scent of fairies and demons along with blood sacrifices and ancient rules concerning when to sow, harvest, and celebrate. And, if they choose, the Burmese Naga can have their souls saved by Buddhist and Christian missionaries.

The monks and the pastors are missionaries, sent by their respective churches to obscure places they certainly wouldn't have visited had it not been for the unrefusable demand of God's administrators. Buddhist missionary Venerable Khema Siri in Makyan, for instance, comes from the Mergui Archipelago on the far side of this large country, a great distance in kilometers and culture from his home.

Nagas, particularly in India, were participants (some might say victims) of "the most massive movement to Christianity in all of Asia, second only to that of the Philippines," according to Richard Eat in *Journal of World History*. Primarily Baptist, the missionaries used a tried and true tactic – translate the Bible into an often invented Roman script form of local languages.

Pastor U Pakun, 30, who lives in Kha Lei, preaches for the Baptist-like Assembly of God. He's bright, enthusiastic, and proudly notes that (in spite of not allowing smoking, drinking, or drugs) he has two hundred eighteen people in his flock. But times are tough; most of his converts became Christian before he arrived in 2010, and in the four years since, he's only had six new converts. It's a numbers game, but he sits cross-legged under a large poster of a classical European-featured Jesus and promises to continue doing his best.

In the four villages we visited, the Baptists and related sects claimed about one quarter of the populations, with the rest following a fuzzy mélange of Animism and Buddhism.

I WOULD MAKE A GOOD MISSIONARY, PROVIDED THE religion pleased me.

The basic choice in choosing a religion is whether you desire a deity who is a Hairy Thunderer or a Cosmic Muffin. I'd opt toward the fluffy, compassionate side of the cosmos, but recognizing that a deity holds power by being unpredictable. Sometimes She acts like a kindly grandmother, offering fresh-from-the-oven chocolate chip cookies, but once in a while, like a high-strung woman having a bad hair day, She causes volcanoes to erupt and important computer documents to disappear. (Perhaps serendipitously, the Nagas, historically at least, don't feel that the Supreme Being must be male.) She is a cosmic Earth Mother, presiding over the sun and rain, the volcanoes and the tides, the maple trees and the mud, the dandelions and the ducks. All-seeing, all-powerful, but too busy with the Blue Sky stuff to worry about day-to-day management. Her name is Sunny.

But Sunny, as a successful Supreme Being, requires a messenger, a prophet to be sure, but one with organizational ability, someone to manage things on Earth. In my religion this would be Hilda, a petite, fire-breathing, Dr. Seuss-quoting redhead with green eyes – cute until cornered, wise beyond her years, generous and forward thinking, with unpredictable magical powers.

Hilda schedules droughts, floods, and plagues. But she also grants outstanding wine vintages, creates iridescent butterflies (Nagas believe dead spirits can transform into Lepidoptera), and gives engineers the skills to design a forgiving golf club that hits the ball cleanly every time yet is legal under R&A rules.

Hilda is Sunny's tough-love administrator and scolds people who cut trees they don't need.

She would be supported by a legion of nymphs, fairies, sprites, and wisps, who enact a full-moon, naked-dancing ritual, supervise the planting of flowers in the forest (because even sprites get bored by monotonous green), and are the patron saints of bingo. Yes, there must be bingo. Thursday nights. Friday nights are when the guys drink beer and play poker.

It would be an animistic faith (waterfall spirits deserve special rituals), with civil admonitions that promote village sanitation, birth control, and education that accepts evolution. It would admonish littering and prohibit playing of loud music (except for the Beach Boys and Verdi); kicking of dogs is verboten. Heavy on rituals and rite-of-passage ceremonies. The religion for which I would be a missionary would be called Temple of Heroic Imposters and Natural Kwirkiness. The theology I'd preach would dump the Ten Commandments and promote just one, all-encompassing admonition: Don't be a jerk. Who determines jerkness? Well, as the appointed emissary of the bureaucracy of this new orthodoxy, I do. I'm a pretty easy-going guy, except when I'm not. Don't push me.

LET'S IMAGINE THE REVERSE: THE FIRST NAGA FROM Myanmar to visit a "more virgin," never-been-visited-by-a-Naga hillside in Arkansas. Let's say the above-mentioned Naga from Myanmar drives up some dirt roads into the Ozark Mountains. The Naga gentleman is accompanied by a traveling companion and a guide. He approaches a dilapidated farmhouse. How quaint – and look, lots of abandoned refrigerators for the naked little kids to play in! He is dressed in Western clothes that are correct but not exactly the style worn by the locals. He doesn't speak English well and relies on his tour guide to translate. How would he be received? Would the local Arkansans welcome him into their home, give him tea, and patiently answer questions about local rituals and migration patterns? Could he poke around the kitchen to see what store-bought goods they had (the easiest way to determine how reliant folks are on a cash economy)? Might he ask to see their ritual masks for rite-of-passage ceremonies? What animal sacrifices they make to ensure a good harvest? What would be the reaction when he asks about politics, and offers small gifts of seeds to the parents and balloons to the kids? And what is their reaction when he asks if he can take a few pictures for his Facebook page?

WESTERNERS HAVE ALWAYS HAD A FASCINATION WITH "primitive cultures." My bookshelf is full of old travelers' tales describing natives, savages, and men just a few degrees more sophisticated than apes.

Consider the name Naga.

The Nagas are sometimes referred to as the "Naked Naga," not simply because in earlier times the men wore loincloths and the women simple skirts and little else, but also as a descriptor of their outsider status in society.

Now consider the "human zoos."

In the second half of the nineteenth century and first half of the twentieth, "human zoos" exhibiting exotic populations were popular attractions in Europe and the United States. The 1889 World's Fair in Paris, visited by twenty-eight million people, displayed four hundred indigenous people, and Colonial Exhibitions in Paris in 1907 and 1931 displayed tribal people in cages, often nude or semi-nude.

At the 1904 World's Fair in St. Louis, "primitives" were displayed to illustrate the bottom end of a "parade of evolutionary progress," the African Pygmies from the exhibition were subsequently displayed in the primate section of the Bronx Zoo. The purpose of the exhibit was twofold: to exhibit the civilizing influence of American rule in the Philippines, which had been obtained from Spain six years earlier (an event that catalyzed Kipling's poem *White Man's Burden*) and to set the stage for economic exploitation of the Philippines' rich natural resources.

For me, this two-barreled approach of demonizing primitive societies and viewing them as less-than-human savages, along with a widely held perception that wilderness is a place of demons, snakes, and disease, sets the stage for wanton environmental destruction worldwide.

Here's my argument.

This dynamic has been going on for as long as technologically developed people have confronted less technologically developed people. During the centuries of European colonial power, the Portuguese, Spanish, Dutch, Belgian, French, Germans, British, and Americans had little compunction against subjugating black and brown folks and taking what they wanted.

Closer to home, consider the "conquering" of the American West. The principle was that the educated and powerful decision-makers from the Eastern seaboard (old, rich, white guys) had a "Manifest Destiny" to civilize the Indians (convert them to Christianity if possible; exterminate them if they refused), slaughter the buffalo, and convert large swathes of wild forests and plains into more productive (and more "civilized") agricultural land.

Today that situation has morphed from white-brown colonialism into brown-brown colonialism. In Asia, for instance, government leaders and businessmen in the lowland cities of Yangon, Jakarta, Kuala Lumpur, Bangkok, Manila, and other capitals have little compunction about being paternalistic toward their naked, darker, less sophisticated brethren in the hills. I've met numerous government ministers who have told me: "We have to help our poor, naked cousins in the forests enjoy what we have." They are, in fact, saying: We who live in the city and are educated, well dressed, speak the national language, and believe in the national religion have a responsibility to help the poor folks in the hills who might lack proper housing, education, sanitation, and – how foolish of them – might not even know all the players of Manchester United. We have a manifest destiny, and opportunity, to give them religion and development. And all we ask in return is that they become good citizens. Oh, one more thing. We don't recognize their land claims for the forest they've been living in for centuries, so we'll go ahead and extract the valuable timber, burn what vegetation remains, and plant oil palm. Don't they dare complain; it's not how civilized people behave. And especially don't complain to foreigners – that's unpatriotic. We're trying to build a nation here.

The implication is that the world is governed by a natural and inevitable progression of cultural development, ranging from the most primitive at the bottom (Naga) to the top of the social totem pole folks (lowlanders in big cities) who epitomize grace, culture, and learning.

So, this arrogance and greed becomes a deadly combination for both traditional culture and the natural environment. It's real, it's prevalent, and it's unstoppable.

Perhaps this "we" vs "them" arrogance toward wilderness partly stems from man's "need-fear" relationship with nature.

On the one hand, we need nature. We come from nature, we are part of nature. This connection is very deep, very ancient, very Jungian in its impact on our collective unconscious. Our very earliest ancestors, before the development of agriculture and writing, even before the wheel and fire when people grovelled with other animals and fought them for carrion, found shelter in the forests, opportunity in the plains. They understood, at least unconsciously, the cycles of rain and drought. Our ancestors came from nature; it was part of them. This may explain why today the presence of green scenery slows our blood pressure and relieves stress. It might explain why people working in bleak, anonymous offices nurture houseplants to brighten things up, and why people recover faster from gall bladder operations when their hospital window has a view of a park (curiously, even having a photograph of nature in the room speeds healing compared to a barren wall).

But what about the fear? We define ourselves partly by what we are not. We are no longer "savages" who co-exist with animals; we are civilized, we have left the darkness. Our ancestors learned to use plants for medicine, build complex shelters, and after much trial and error, to dominate nature by mastering fire, making metal tools, growing crops, and domesticating other animals. We became the masters of the universe. We have civilization, language, Michelangelo and Michael Jackson and Michael Jordan. We have ploughs and guns, bicycles and cell phones. Many of us have been imprinted by one of the three strict, paternalistic, monotheistic desert religions that put a lot more emphasis on us having "dominion" over nature than on, say, the Buddhist approach of living in "harmony" with nature. That's why we're uncomfort-able when "undisciplined" nature approaches too close. We manicure our gardens and kill crabgrass to "manage" nature. That's why the Balinese file the teeth of their pre-adolescent children – so that the child does not have pointy, animal-like cuspids. That's why most first- and second-generation urban people, like those you'll find in Yangon, for instance, will look at me askance when I explain that I'm going into the deep forests. I'm likely to get a response like, "Ugh, full of snakes!" or "No electricity" or "Go shopping in Bangkok instead." It's all a way of saying "the forest is alien, it's dangerous, it's filled with dusky people with rough hands having strange animistic beliefs who worship spirits that reside in the trees and streams and volcanoes." There are creatures in the deep wilderness (think yeti) that will tear off your head. We're afraid of looking too deeply into the mirror and seeing our wild side.

This is near to the core of our schizophrenic relationship with nature. We need nature but we fear it. We're part of nature but we want to dissociate ourselves from anything too wild. On one side we have what could be termed a female/yin approach to nature – we are part of the global scheme of things, the interwoven tapestry of life that is mysterious, complex, sharing, questioning, supportive, fertile. On the other hand we are very male/yang – logical, goal-driven, suspicious of outsiders, confident, potent. Conquerors.

IN HIS 1939 BOOK *THE NAKED NAGAS*, AN ANTHROPOLOGIST with the suitably exotic name of Christoph von Fürer-Haimendorf liberally illustrates daily life in a Naga village with photos of comely young women who live up to the title of his scholarly book. He carefully records how "the youngest – and naturally often the prettiest – girls wear their hair quite closely cropped. This is a sign that they are virgins, or at least are taken for such." He then advises the reader that "the average Naga girl soon grows weary of her premarital state, her short hair, and her virginity" and enters into a casual trial marriage; such relationships "seldom last long and are usually dissolved in the most peaceful way." (He also notes that the "magical current" that is released during clandestine trysts held in rice granaries enhances the vigor of the seed rice stored in the shed, but that's another story.) "Perhaps it is the fear that the girl may die without love experience, which is responsible for this strange custom," von Fürer-Haimendorf tells us. "Virginity wins no halo in the Naga heaven, but is regarded rather as a sin, for has not the deceased failed to fulfill the duties of her earthly life?" The ex-virgin, he explains, then returns to society, lets her hair grow, and seeks a more lasting union. The young man, meanwhile,

> boasts of his first love affair by decorating his black loincloth with three rows of pure white cowrie shells, while a Don Juan, succeeding either in seducing a married woman or in carrying on a simultaneous love affair with two sisters, proudly adds a fourth string of cowrie shells to his loincloth.

WHEN WE WALKED INTO KHA LEI, ONE OF OUR "FIRST contact" villages, the few people who weren't at the farms scattered, seeking refuge in their houses from where they could safely watch our progress. Who knows what they thought? Adults and toddlers alike behaved the same, scampering away, but curious.

The next day things changed.

We walked around the village with the head man and the shaman. We visited the basketmaker and the old lady who knows about medicinal plants and the headman's grandson, who is prepared, perhaps even keen, to take over when his grandfather dies. We gave small presents – my traveling stash includes packets of vegetable seeds, reading glasses for the old folks, multi-purpose tools, some Buddhist amulets, and postcards from home of which photos of snow-covered mountains always generate discussion. Not quite the trading of beads and mirrors offered by gold- and nutmeg-seeking European explorers, but more in the nature of small presents to thank people for letting us wander around their village and drink rice wine in their homes. But actually we do the same anywhere in the world – if you're invited to someone's house for dinner, you bring flowers or wine or cheesecake. A few folks mimed taking a photo and asked why we didn't have a Kodak. Well, we had been reluctant to wander around the village snapping photos but indeed, we did have Kodaks tucked away in our backpacks. We politely asked if we might take some pictures of ourselves with our hosts and promised to send the photos back (which we have done, via Saw Hla Chit who returned some months later).

During our walkabout a group of young women shyly monitored our progress. After a few hours of watching us make small talk with the older men and women, the bolder of the teenage girls stepped up. They too wanted portraits taken by the foreigners.

Timid at first, Wi Thwe, 18, her friends, the sisters Pa Phaw, 20, and Wi Phaw, 17, asked Saw Hla Chit whether the strange (or good-looking?) foreigners could take their picture. The girls ran inside their houses to change and returned in formal Naga dress, with strings of old yellow beads and mostly-black handwoven costumes. Snap snap snap. Have a look at the little screen on the back of the camera. Giggle, giggle. Then they ran inside again, only to emerge minutes later wearing modern Burmese clothes – blue jeans and a red floral top. In a way it felt like a *Vogue* shoot with Kim Kardashian, except the Naga girls kept their breasts well hidden and had probably paid only a few dollars for their outfits.

I noted that the girls, all wearing long hair, were in a hurry to try on as many different outfits as possible before the light ran out. But we wanted a relationship, at least a conversation.

Pa Phaw shyly explained that she had finished secondary school in Khamti, and her sister Wi Phaw had completed her primary school in the smaller town of Lahe. Both wistfully said they'd rather live in town than up in the hills.

Their friend and leader of the fashion brigade, Wi Thwe, completed "a few years" at secondary school in the town of Lahe. She expressed having her share of problems – she's an orphan and has a glass eye due to an infection at age six when she went to distant Mandalay for treatment. Wi Thwe worries whether she will find a husband who can overlook her deformity.

Without encouragement, the girls posed with hand gestures that would be recognizable to any user of Instagram anywhere in the world: the two-fingered V sign, along with exaggerated angular postures, leaning against each other, making the heart sign with their hands or arms. Snap snap. Then they repeated the process with another quick change, this time a pink shirt with pink pants and a blue Chinese-style dress for another round of photos.

Farquhar and I asked how they got their fashion sense. "It just happened," Wi Thwe suggested, this time wearing a black T-shirt with black jeans. She doesn't feel she is fashionable; she's just a village girl, she said, perhaps implying that we should disagree and praise her sophistication. "Not at all," I said. "You've got good taste in clothes and look terrific." The girls explained that they see magazines and go to town for weddings and festivals. They watch TV. "Where?" we ask. "At the monastery," one girl says. Like our friend Khema Siri in Makyan, the Buddhist monk at Kha Lei also shows Burmese pop music videos to attract acolytes; once he has them well and truly entertained by the flash and glitter of modern life, he can lecture them about the Four Noble Truths.

Eventually the light becomes too dim for decent photos. We promise to return the following morning for another photo session. My main thoughts were: what a wonderful invention digital photography is. And how quickly so-called isolated, so-called rural, so-called-simple people adopt and adapt.

WE HAD A BRIEF CONVERSATION, BUT I DON'T CLAIM TO understand anything about the lives of these girls. What dynamics run their daily lives? Do they believe in an afterlife? Do they worry about the future? Do they celebrate birthdays? Did they have rites of passage? Is my ten-day-old beard a mark of desirable masculinity or a nosy old guy's aberration?

Put another way, are we fundamentally different or are we like-minded citizens of a global village? Is there a basic belief-chasm between American and Naga, between urban and rural, between people who understand a written culture and folks who are comfortable with an oral culture?

THERE ARE HUNDREDS OF NAGA VILLAGES TO EXPLORE, and if I were to trek deeper into the rugged territory, no doubt I would enter even more "more virgin" villages. But I'm seeking new pastures, and my next trip will be to southern Chin State to visit folks of a sub-group of the Shan group. No airport, no roads. I will need to fly to Sittwe (the city where Muslims and Buddhists have been battering each other), take a boat upriver one day, then a car for half a day, then a second boat for another day, and then start walking. Saw Hla Chit promises me these settlements are "double more virgin." For that visit I'm going to try a new tactic. I'll try to shut up a bit and encourage my new friends to ask me questions. Who knows what they'll ask. What is your work? How many children do you have? How many chickens/pigs/goats do you own and how many rice crops do you harvest each year? How many days to walk from your village to ours? What is your religion? (a tricky one that will no doubt morph into a follow-up: How can you not have a religion?) And the question I both welcome and dread. What are you doing here?

ABOUT THE AUTHOR

Paul on the Ayeryawaddy, near Katha.

PAUL SPENCER SOCHACZEWSKI has written *Share Your Journey, An Inordinate Fondness for Beetles, The Sultan and the Mermaid Queen, Redheads, Soul of the Tiger* (co-authored with Jeff McNeely), and other acclaimed books, along with some six hundred bylined articles in leading international publications. He has lived and worked in more than eighty countries, including long stints in Southeast Asia.

Visit Paul at:
www.sochaczewski.com